"We live in a world that c̲_____ and yet so available within ʒ̲ʒ̲ ʒ̲ʒ̲ʒ̲ʒ̲ ʒ̲ʒ̲ʒ̲ ʒ̲ʒ̲ʒ̲ʒ̲ʒ̲ʒ̲ ʒ̲ʒ̲ ʒ̲ʒ̲_ Karen Sebastian explains from experience the enormity of the possible when hope seems dim regarding wandering children. She has the gratitude of shepherds like me who are always grateful to relay lessons of 'hope' that exceeds all expectations and which brings 'peace' that passes understanding."
~ JACK W. HAYFORD, Author and Founding Pastor
The Church on the Way, and Chancellor of The King's University

"Travel with Karen Sebastian as she takes you on a life journey, traversing down treacherous pathways and learning through her experiences how to find the joy and peace that comes from trusting God in your darkest hours. Her refreshing honesty opens your mind and heart to insights that will equip you to face your own life journey. Karen will help you see life through the eyes of HOPE!"
~ JANELLE HAIL, Founder/CEO
National Breast Cancer Foundation, Inc.

"The compelling message of hope that is shared in this vital book is one that Karen not only teaches, but lives . . . everyday. Whether coaching in the business marketplace or teaching seminars, her spiritual insight, practical wisdom and sensitivity to the Holy Spirit's desire to heal the broken and wounded are inspirational. Corrie Ten Boom said, "there is no pit so deep that the love of God does not go deeper still." You will find the truths in The Power of Hope for Prodigals to be those that have power to go deeply within to set you and/or your loved-one free."
~ KIM VASTINE, Founder and President
Ambassador Alliance International

"Few people have the gift of putting their deepest experiences into words. Karen Sebastian obviously has a God-given gift! Not only has Karen experienced the presence of Christ in many of life's most trying circumstances, she has also written a book of hope which will help all of us cope with life's challenges. I fully recommend The Power of Hope not only to parents, but to any serious reader desiring real guidance toward a peace-filled life."
~ DR. SIDNEY WESTBROOK, Professor
Christ for the Nations Institute

THE POWER OF
HOPE
FOR PRODIGALS

PREPARE THE WAY HOME

KAREN SEBASTIAN

Harris
House
Publishing

Published by Harris House Publishing
Arlington, Texas
USA

This title is also available in other formats.

Cover by Christopher Flynn
Cover photo © Davidmartyn | Dreamstime.com
Author's photo by Hannah Cheatheam

Library of Congress Cataloging-in-Publication Data

Sebastian, Karen.
     The Power of Hope for Prodigals: Prepare the Way Home / Karen Sebastian
          p.cm.
     ISBN 978-0-9824160-4-4 (pbk.)
     1. Parent and Child. 2. Parenting—Religious Aspects.
     3. Hope—Religious Aspects. I. Title
HQ75585.S43   2012

                                      2012934714

Dedication

I dedicate this book to my mother,
Betty Pritchett, who was a champion intercessor.
She taught me through her unselfish example
how to pray fervently and 'without ceasing' for
others. Now that she moved to Heaven I think
what I miss most is her sweet voice on the phone
asking me how she should pray. I am eternally
grateful that she taught me there is always hope
no matter how dark the situation seems.

Acknowledgements

I want to thank my wonderful family for their prayer support through the tough years described in this book. I know that we can share this testimony because of your faithful prayers.

For my husband, Bill: Thank you for your patience and unswerving faith that this book would not only be written but actually finished. Your steadfast example and love for your family leaves a legacy of the Heavenly Father's love for us.

To my parents, Bill and Betty Pritchett: My earliest memories are waking up to your prayers. You consistently modeled a spiritual walk of prayer and the Word of God.

To my mother-in-love, Edith Sebastian (Nana): You had such a special bond with Elizabeth, and I know you prayed for her and all your grandchildren every day.

To Uncle Bill Gilbert: Despite your rough cowboy exterior, I know you prayed for our kids many hours every day.

To my sister, Linda Richey: I always knew you were just a phone call away. Thank you for consistently listening and encouraging me.

To my children: Elizabeth, I appreciate your candor, strength, and courage. Megan, I cherish your consistent expression of love and efforts to be a peacemaker. Sean, I admire your pursuit of truth through revisiting painful memories and seeking to gain the Lord's perspective.

To our sweet Praise Unlimited Church family: Thank you for loving us no matter what happened and showing our children how special they are.

To Lynn Scarborough: Thank you for helping me take the first steps in putting together the outline and basic structure of the book. You are amazingly generous.

To Terry Harris and Harris House Publishing: Your skillful editing guided and encouraged me to keep going. You are a very special gift.

Contents

I wrote the following song for my oldest daughter in the midst of her prodigal journey.

Elizabeth's Song

I feel so sad today
My daughter's gone away
I don't know how to reach her
Don't know where she's gone.
I wonder, what's her pain?
And why things aren't the same?
As when she was a little bundle
Looking at the world in wonder?

[Chorus]

Lord, keep her safe and sound
Send extra angels all around
Protect her from the evil one
Who wants to take her life.
I call on You today
Please help her find her way
And bring her back home safe
She'll always have a place … in my heart.

How did it come to this?
When did she start to drift?
It happened very slowly
Yet she seems out of reach.
And how can she now know
We really love her so
And want her to succeed in life
And have a future that is bright?

[Repeat Chorus]

Introduction

*Prepare the way of the Lord; make straight in
the desert a highway for our God. Every valley shall
be exalted and every mountain and hill brought low.
The crooked places shall be made straight and the rough
places smooth. The glory of the Lord shall be revealed.*
Isaiah 40:3-5

The distinguished gentleman stood, squinting under the bright sunlight. Shading his eyes with one hand, he focused on a figure approaching the gates of the city. "Could that be my son? Oh, dear God, please let it be him," he yearned silently. As the disheveled young man neared, their eyes met for one brief second before the younger man looked away. The older gentleman's face fell. Every day he came to sit at the gates, his eyes searching the crowds of people who approached the city. As the sunlight faded, he would walk home, his shoulders slumped in sadness. Yet each new day he resumed his search with hope and confidence that his lost son would come home.

This is how I imagine the father of the prodigal as he waited for his wayward son to return. Scripture tells us that when he saw his son coming home, he ran to him and embraced him. He told the servants to prepare a party to celebrate this son who was lost but had now come home. He had been expecting him to return and was ready and waiting to throw that party. Nowhere does it mention a discussion of past problems. He did not yell, "It's about time you got home! Do you realize what you've put us through?" Instead, he welcomed him with tenderness and love.

You probably picked up this book because you either have a prodigal, know someone who does, or fear your strong-willed child could become one. The details don't matter. I've purposely left out certain details of what my own daughter Elizabeth went through. What does matter is the message of hope that is applicable at every stage. Hope changed the atmosphere of our home. With confidence in the promises of the Lord, I began to see my prodigal daughter how the Father saw her.

My prayer is that, as you read the words of this book and pray the scripturally-based prayers at the end of each chapter, your own sense of hope will be restored. I would love to put my arms around you and personally pray with you. Remember, our Heavenly Father once was separated from His beloved Son. He knows your pain. He also knows the beginning from the end, and He will restore your hope in His purposes for your family. In fact, as your hope returns and grows, you too can start planning a welcome home party.

Do I have to go on this trip?

The soft rhythmic breathing of my husband starkly contrasted the wild worries racing through my head. How could he sleep at a time like this? Frustrated by my anxious thoughts, I donned my robe and stumbled down the hallway. It had been two long weeks of sleepless nights, and tonight was no different. Our daughter Elizabeth had stormed out of the house one evening, and we had not heard a word from her. We called all her friends to no avail, and after reporting her as a runaway, there was not much more we could do. To numb the fear and despair, I sat on the sofa and reached for the remote. I blinked against the bright blue light as the TV came on, but realizing a special newscast was airing, I forced my eyes to focus. The newscaster's grim face matched my own. A serial rapist in the city was targeting young female runaways. "Oh, dear Lord, please keep my baby safe," I cried out. I clicked the TV off and walked to the kitchen where I collapsed on a chair and wept.

I considered venturing out to look for Elizabeth. I had an idea where she might be. In the days before she disappeared, I had overheard a phone conversation with a 'new' friend. "Okay, I'll meet you later tonight." I didn't mean to eavesdrop, but lately I had been worried about Elizabeth. I was horrified to think that she wanted to go to an area of Dallas that, at that time, was known for its clubs, bars, tattoo shops, and piercing parlors. Every weekend hundreds of young people hung out there.

Recently, Elizabeth's style had changed drastically. She now dressed in black from head to toe. Black lips and nails accentuated her stark white makeup, and she outlined her eyes with heavy black eyeliner.

The changes had been gradual at first, and I struggled not to overreact. Other parents advised us to choose our battles, but now I was frightened to see that Elizabeth had pulled out all restraints. She was going for shock value in her appearance and behavior. A few external things wouldn't have been so bad, but she was hanging out with the wrong crowd. I feared for her physical safety, but mostly her spiritual condition.

The methodical tick-tock of the kitchen clock brought me back to the current crisis. I glanced at the time. It was two in the morning. An avalanche of emotions swept over me and I began to sob. "How did we end up in this situation?" I cried. "Why, Lord? Oh Lord, please show me why? What did we do wrong, Lord?"

As I gave vent to my pent up emotions and despair, I actually felt worse. A deep sense of personal failure overwhelmed me. "How could this be happening to us? We did all the right things," I vented.

Devoted to full-time ministry, my husband and I had dedicated Elizabeth to the Lord from her earliest days. We taught her Biblical principles, regularly prayed for her, and surrounded her with love. She received Jesus as her Savior at an early age and was nurtured in the things of the Lord.

"Where did we go wrong?" I continued to sob as hopelessness enveloped me like a dark cloud.

PAINT A PICTURE OF HOPE

Slowly, I realized I could cry no more. I was at a complete end of myself. My stomach ached. My throat and chest hurt. My strength was gone. At that moment, I would have gladly sent in my resignation letter as a parent if I could have found the address to put on the envelope.

"Why, Lord, just tell me why?" I moaned.

The Lord spoke to my heart in a very special way that night. While it was not an audible voice, it was a clear message nonetheless.

I'm giving you a testimony.

I shook my head in disbelief. Was this just me?

"A testimony?" I questioned.

Dry your tears and go to sleep. I'm giving you a testimony that will bless many because they will see My power at work in you and in your daughter. It will be a testimony of My love.

"What do you want me to do?"

Paint her a picture of hope, was the reply.

"How do I paint a picture of hope?"

Begin to see her the way that I see her. Show her how much I love her.

"But I'm so angry," I replied bitterly. "I just see someone who is messing up her life and, in the process, bringing all of us down." At that moment, God's search light
turned my way. All my attention up to that point had
focused on what needed to change in Elizabeth, but suddenly I realized that change needed to start in me.

Begin to see her the way that I see her.

With a newfound humility, I prayed, "Dear Lord,
please let me see Elizabeth the way You see her." In my
mind's eye, I began to see a vision of my daughter. This
was more than I could have created myself. She was
standing with her face lifted toward Heaven. The angry,
hardened expression was gone and her face was radiant.
Tears streamed down her cheeks as she expressed her love
for God. She sang a beautiful song of praise.

Reaching out to the Lost

When I saw the joy on Elizabeth's face as she wor-
shipped the Lord in my vision, I gained a perspective of
how our Heavenly Father saw my daughter. I began to
sense the deep unconditional love He has toward all of
us. He looked past all the external trappings of rebellion
and saw what I had not been willing to see. He saw a lost

lamb filled with fears, anxiety, disappointments, despair, and a need to belong. With greater insight into His heart, I envisioned Jesus' parable of the lost sheep in a whole new way. If I could fill in the details, I imagine it would go something like this . . .

The tired shepherd leads the sheep to the stall where they can rest for the night. Glancing at the setting sun, he looks longingly toward the house where his family gathers for their evening meal. He has been looking forward to this special time. He enters the gate and calls the sheep to follow him. He starts counting as they come through the gate. Ninety-seven, ninety-eight, ninety-nine. His heart sinks as he realizes that one of the little lambs is missing. He stops by the house to tell them he is going to find the lost lamb.

The good shepherd immediately leaves the ninety-nine who had the good sense to follow him in order to go after the one who lost its way. He thinks of all the times he has had to rescue the lambs who can't handle their freedom. Setting out in the dark, he returns to the places they had been that day. He calls out and then listens intently for the bleating of the scared little lamb. He is compassionate rather than angry. He knows that the lamb is defenseless against predators if he leaves it out there all night. The wind is picking up and starting to howl. Others would give up on the one since ninety-nine were safe, but not this shepherd. He is determined to find this lamb and his persistence pays off. Finally, he hears the soft bleating and finds the shivering lamb whose hoof is stuck between two rocks. Tenderly, he stoops down and holds the lamb close until it calms down. Then he throws it over his shoulder and takes it home.

"I found the lost lamb!" he exclaims to his waiting family as he enters his house.

"We knew you would!" they respond. "Let's have a party!" Everyone rejoices with him because he rescued the one who was lost.

CHANGING MY PERSPECTIVE

I had been focusing on how desperate I felt and what others would think rather than preparing the road home for Elizabeth. With one glimpse of the Father's perspective, I was ready to move into a new dimension of hope.

Paint her a picture of hope, the Lord impressed on my heart as He let me see through His lens. Right now Elizabeth could not see past her current situation. I was the one who could establish a background of hope. Our current situation was not the end. God had a plan. Good things were ahead for us all. I asked Him to imprint His vision of Elizabeth on my mind. I would need it for the days ahead. What a difference hope makes!

Taking a deep breath, I held it for a moment and then exhaled slowly. The tension in my stomach began to relax. Slowly I realized the pain in my chest was gone. I felt peace for the first time since Elizabeth had taken her detour. A great sense of hope filled my heart. Yes, she had lost her way, but this was not her final destination. She was on a dark road, but her loving Father would be with her every step of the way. God wasn't afraid of the dark places she frequented. His light would dispel the darkness. I could trust Him to work in her life. He loved her more than I could even imagine, and He was completing the good work He had begun in her.

A miracle began that night, and it started with me. I was no longer stumbling in the dark. For the first time in months, I felt hope. I wasn't sure what would happen next, but a renewed sense of purpose enveloped me. I started to cry again, but this time they were tears of joy. My heart was beginning to thaw. I wanted to love Elizabeth the way her Heavenly Father loved her. With that kind of love, nothing she could do would make me stop loving her. Good was going to come out of this experience. God had a purpose and plan. He was giving us a testimony that would allow us to share His power and love.

You are probably reading this book because someone you love is like the lamb that lost its way. When this happens, we also can feel lost, hopeless, and afraid. All our efforts to fix the situation seem to make it worse. The Lord shares how He feels about those who lose their way. The shepherd in His story must have been tired from a long day of caring for the flock, yet immediately he left the others to look for the one stray. Every single one of us can lose our way at one time or another. It is a great comfort to know that the Lord actively pursues us, finds us, and rejoices when we come home.

Let's travel together through this difficult time. Take it from someone who's been there and survived— you will make it through. Continue to believe that God is working in your child's life even when you do not see it. A deep work is taking place, and you can have peace knowing that God always does a good job.

Hope Tools

Hope LENS

Your perspective can change as you choose to look through a lens of hope. Hope sheds light on desperate situations by providing context for a brighter future ahead.

Let go of your agenda. We block the incoming light of hope in our lives when we become discouraged because life has not worked out according to our plans. As we try harder and harder to rearrange the circumstances of our lives and manipulate the decisions of others, we find ourselves in a dark place filled with disappointment. Often our children interpret our reactions as being their fault. Even when their behavior is disturbing and scary, focus on what God is doing and trust that He is working even when you don't see anything on the outside.

Envision your child the way our Heavenly Father sees her. It can be hard to do when she rolls her eyes and mouths off sarcastically. Transform the way you see your children by taking a step back and applying the truth of God's plan for their lives. If you are currently dismayed at the direction they are headed in, reframe the situation. Speak words of hope because you are confident that God will turn all things around for good. Lessons can be learned and insights gained even in failure. God looks past all the external trappings and sees what's going on inside. His perspective makes a huge difference and can help you see past the surface into hurts, disappointments, and pain.

Nurture hope when all seems lost. This is not the time to give up; instead, paint a picture of hope. In order to do this, allow God to change your perspective first. This change will be reflected in the way you speak to your child and how you interact with her or him. God's hope is much more than wishful thinking. His hope means that even when things are not where we want them to be, He is in control. He is working, and the future will be good.

Shift your focus. Paralyzed by fear and regret, I had relinquished my power to choose and to move forward because of my daughter's decisions. Hopelessness grows when you concentrate on situations over which you have no control. Instead, focus on the one area you *can* control—your own attitude. It is possible to find peace in the midst of difficult circumstances.

PRAYER

Lord, I welcome You into this difficult situation. Thank You for giving me the blessing of parenting _____ and giving me Your wisdom as You work in her/his life. I need Your reassurance that _____ will come home to You and to her/his family. I leave the timing to You, and I will prepare my heart to receive her/him whenever that happens. Please give me the gift of hope that overflows and abounds (Romans 15:13). Thank You for the testimony that we will have to help others. I now see that my part will be to prepare the way through consistent hope-filled prayer and creating an atmosphere where hope can grow.

Show me how You see _____. I release my current view of her/him and ask You to fill me with joy and peace as I wait for You to complete the work You have started (Phil. 1:6). With Your guidance, I get out of the way of Your work in her/his life. I choose to stop interfering by imposing my ideas and pressure to do things my way.

I thank You, Lord, that You haven't moved. You are still in charge and are aware of what is going on in _____'s life (Psalms 11:4-6). May she/he know the truth because the truth will set her/him free (John 8:32). As she/he is set free, she/he will recognize the road home is short. May _____ love the Lord with all her/his heart and with all her/his soul and with all her/his mind (Matthew 22:37). In Jesus name, Amen.

Hope Expressions

May the God of hope fill you with all joy and peace as you trust in him, so that you may overflow with hope by the power of the Holy Spirit.
                    Romans 15:13

PREPARE THE WAY HOME

Taking Detours

"I hate you!" Elizabeth screamed as she slammed the door to her room. She locked the door and cranked up the music to a deafening volume. "Just leave me alone! Go away!" she screamed. "You are so mean!"

I had just told Elizabeth that she was grounded and could not go out, but I felt like the one who was being punished. Leaning against the door with a heavy sigh, I slowly slid to the floor. I could feel the bass notes vibrating the door against my back as the lyrics blasted out expletives. Elizabeth sang along at the top of her lungs.

A familiar pattern had emerged in our interactions as the verbal sparring escalated, and we made no progress. Elizabeth knew how to push my buttons—especially with her lack of respect. Much of her response centered on how unfair we were to her and how much she hated her life. The negative scenario played in an endless loop during this difficult period of our lives.

We were dealing with anger issues on both sides, but I made every attempt to be more understanding. My biggest challenge was to avoid overreacting. I never knew I was capable of so much anger. She seemed to have an uncanny ability to sense my imbalance and push in that direction. It was exhausting and frightening. I was never more aware of the weaknesses and flaws in my own character.

We had drifted so far apart. I was concerned for our relationship. How could I speak hope to her when I could hardly speak a civil word? There just had to be a better way to pull her back, to reason with her, to change things back to the way they were supposed to be. She kept taking steps down the wrong path and nothing we did seemed to improve the situation. In fact, the more we pushed, the more determined she seemed to keep going in the wrong direction. I would let my imagination run wild as I projected where this path could take her.

One particular night as these dire scenarios played out in my head, a fitful sleep finally came. In a vivid dream, I saw my beautiful daughter covered in tattoos and piercings. I screamed at her, "What is wrong with you? Are you trying to give me a nervous breakdown? I can't take any more of this."

The next day, as I was flipping through channels, a daytime talk show caught my attention. The guests were parents whose teenage children were totally covered in tattoos. In the 1990s when this took place, such body art was considered repulsive by mainstream society. One of the boys had shaved and tattooed his head. His mother and father had kicked the young man out of their home and said they wanted nothing more to do with him. The parents ranted and raved. They were screaming and crying. Their kids walked away from them and stood next to a man sitting across the studio.

As I started to change the channel, the camera zoomed in on the man surrounded by teens. Tattoos covered his entire body. His tongue had been cut in two parts so that it looked like that of a serpent. He spoke deliberately, punctuating each phrase by thrusting his tongue out like a snake. "I'll take in every kid that you kick out. So go ahead, send them my way." He reached over and hugged one of the young people.

That's when it hit me. What these young people craved was love and acceptance. Elizabeth wanted me to love her just the way she was. Could I provide her with this level of acceptance? There was only one way to do this. I had to allow God's love to fill me so completely that I gained His perspective of her. Clearly, I had forgotten the definition of a detour—an indirect or roundabout path used temporarily. The key word is 'temporarily.' Elizabeth was not going to stay there. And even if she did—I still loved her.

The next morning I hugged Elizabeth affectionately. She stiffened immediately and said, "What are you doing? What do you want?"

"I want you to know I love you," I told her. I wanted to keep talking but instead chose to keep my mouth shut. I remembered the man on the talk show who was hugging the kids whose parents had kicked them out. As I hugged her, I wanted her to feel my unconditional love and acceptance. Slowly, Elizabeth relaxed in my arms. She hugged me back. We had both taken a step in the right direction.

I was able to flip the Hope Switch by viewing Elizabeth's current situation as a detour rather than a destination. It was not my job to put her in a prison and watch her like a warden. Instead, it was my job to pray for her every day with prayers of hope. My responsibility was to paint her a picture of hope.

A background of hope, as I discovered, is rooted in love rather than fear. I had been so afraid of her mistakes that I had lost sight of the truth that God loved her more than I did. She did not need the threat of punishment to stay in line. God was working from the inside out and would accomplish His plan for her. It was not up to me to get her on the right path. 1 John 4:18 says, "There is no fear in love. But perfect love drives out fear, because fear has to do with punishment. The one who fears is not made perfect in love." It was my job to create an environment where she saw God's love in action.

This difficult season was a temporary detour, and I could trust the good plans the Lord had for our family. We were headed in the right direction—it just might take us a little longer to get there. In fact, these detours could become an adventure.

Hope Tools

Here are a few activities that I discovered as I looked for ways to 'paint a picture of hope' for our daughter. They gave me joy and brought laughter. I trust they will inspire you as you share hope with your child.

HOPE STATEMENTS

Make a list of all the qualities you love about your child. Make sure that they are not innate or something they were born with such as their good looks. For example: You are very good at working with children. You are such a good friend to others.

Put a positive spin or approach on the challenging parts of your child's personality or approach to life. For example instead of stubborn—determined and confident of what they want.

Keep this list accessible so you can review it on a regular basis. Then affirm your child at least once a day. When you can't think of something good to say, pull out the list to remind yourself of your child's good qualities.

HOPE DESTINATIONS

Engage in hope destination conversations. Here are some possible questions to get the conversation going:

What kind of work would you enjoy doing when you are older?

What are you passionate about?

What do you really like to do?

What would it take to get there?

Follow up with specific steps to help her/him move toward the right destination.

STORIES

"I'll never forget the overwhelming sense of love that I felt the first time I held you in my arms," I told Elizabeth.

"Uh huh…" she mumbled. "You picked me up at the airport and I was only eleven hours old," she recited with a roll of her eyes.

"I know you've heard it a thousand times before, but I never get tired of telling you what a miracle you are and how blessed we are to have you in our lives," I continued. "There I stood with a diaper bag over my shoulder and everyone had gotten off the plane except for our friends."

"Yeah, and he came out with a blanket over one arm," she retorted.

"I want you to know how very blessed we were when they placed you in our arms. It was love at first sight," I told her. "And that will never, ever change." She looked up briefly, and for a second I thought I saw moisture in her eyes.

"What about Dad?" she asked with a tiny smile.

"Well, Dad only had to take one look at you and you had him," I beamed. "Your little pinkie wrapped right around his heart and you could have pretty much anything you wanted from that point on."

For a period of time, I stopped telling the stories of the sense of awe I felt as I walked into the airport with empty arms and walked out with a beautiful baby girl in my arms. Her dad had called everyone we knew to tell them all about his little girl.

As I resurrected the hope in my own heart, I realized that we had stopped talking about the good times. Things may be tough right now, but wonderful memories can bring smiles to your faces and reconnect your hearts.

CREATIVE OUTLETS

In my despair over Elizabeth, my creativity dried up. I felt like I was trudging through each day in lead-filled boots. Miraculously, my creativity quickly returned after I accepted the possibility of hope and change. The words and melody of a song for Elizabeth came to me like a stream. You can find the words to the song in the front of this book on page 11. What had changed? I had. My situation was the same. At that point, I didn't know where my daughter was, yet I was humming a new melody of hope—"She'll always have a place in my heart." Creativity awakened the truth of what I was feeling in ways that could only emerge through a song. What is one of your creative outlets through which God's hope can flow?

TREASURE HUNTS

"What in the world are you doing?" said Elizabeth when she saw me surrounded by boxes of pictures at the kitchen table.

"This is my new project," I answered.

"Looks like a mess to me!" she responded with a smirk on her face.

I ignored her sarcasm and kept looking at the pictures. I couldn't stop smiling as I remembered all the good times.

"Hey, is that me when I was a baby?" she asked.

"Yes, it is. Look at how little you were!" I told her. "That's your baby dedication with Pastor Ron in Orange, California. Just look at Dad's face—he was beaming the whole time!"

It was a magical moment that transported us for a few moments to a happier time and place. Finances were tight, so I needed a way to put together an inexpensive scrapbook or treasure book as I like to call it. I purchased sheet protectors, put them in binders, and started sorting the pictures. I'd pull out the boxes of pictures when we were together. It was a neutral zone where I escaped from the pressures of our volatile relationship. We reconnected in those brief moments by talking about the good times.

Think about the funny anecdotes and experiences when your child was little. As you look through those pictures, talk about the vacation, kindergarten graduation, or best friend in grade school. This can build a bridge that allows you to reconnect on a loving level and breaks down barriers between you.

Prayer

Thank You, Heavenly Father, that You have a destiny and a purpose for _____ (Jeremiah 29:11). Right now, it's hard to see any progress, yet I know that nothing takes You by surprise. I thank You for showing me Your perspective as You work out this situation in a way that provides hope and a prosperous future. I receive Your peace in this situation and release my child to You. You say that You will keep me in perfect peace when I keep my mind focused on You (Isaiah 26:2). I choose to take my focus off my child and place it on You. I run to Your arms for comfort, peace, and shelter during this detour.

I acknowledge that You are working at a deep level to draw _____ to Your ways. I am grateful that Your love is eternal and that You will not quit working in her/his life (Psalm 144:7-8 MSG). _____ has not gone so far that she/he cannot come back to what You have planned for her/him. You have an amazing way of taking broken pieces and creating something beautiful (Psalm 18:20). This detour does not determine her/his identity. No influence or group of friends is more important than You. Thank You, Lord, for protecting _____ from trouble. You have shielded her/him on all sides and lifted her/his head (Psalm 3:3). Even as _____ faces the current crisis, she/he is waking up to the truth that all she/he has to do is turn to You. You are more willing to work on her/his behalf than she/he can even imagine.

Surround _____ with songs of deliverance (Psalm 32:7). It has been a tough night, but I thank You that we can look forward to joy and laughter in the morning (Psalm 30:5). This laughter is healing our family from the inside out and is restoring our balance and purpose (Proverbs 17:22). We know that You are working and that You have a purpose for us as a family as well as individually (Ephesians 3:20). We rejoice in anticipating what You are going to do in and through us.

In Jesus' name, Amen.

Hope Expressions

For I know the plans I have for you," declares the LORD, "plans to prosper you and not to harm you, plans to give you hope and a future.
                                    Jeremiah 29:11

Removing Roadblocks

"Elizabeth, you're grounded for the weekend. We just got a call from school saying that you've been skipping classes," I told her firmly.

"I hate that stupid school. I hate this stupid family. I hate you!" screamed Elizabeth. She ran down the hall and slammed her bedroom door.

My heart sank. I looked up at my husband with tears in my eyes. In that moment, the peacemaker in our home reached the end of his patience. Rarely did my gentle husband get ruffled enough to show his anger. Now he stomped down the hallway yelling, "You are not going to talk to your mother that way! What is wrong with you?"

I ran into the bathroom and collapsed to my knees, weeping. I was so weary of the battles and sick with worry about where this situation was taking our family. From down the hallway, I could hear their irate voices intensify. My husband's tone was livid. I couldn't remember him ever sounding this angry. It scared me. I ran back to the bedroom and was shocked when I saw that things had escalated to the point he had her by the throat as she pushed against him.

"Both of you stop right now before someone gets hurt!" I screamed.

My husband immediately dropped his hand and left the room. I followed him into the kitchen where he picked up the phone. He slumped over in defeat. Tears coursed down his face.

"What are you doing?" I asked anxiously.

"I'm calling the police," he replied. He proceeded to report what had just happened.

Elizabeth walked into the kitchen and said sarcastically, "What are you doing now?"

"I just called the police," he said quietly.

"That figures. You just had to go call the cops on me, didn't you? I hate you!" she screamed.

"I called the cops on *me*," he answered.

Elizabeth's mouth dropped as he explained to us his reasoning. She started crying and exclaimed, "Call them back and tell them they don't need to come. I'm sorry," she said as her eyes filled with tears.

A resounding knock on the door interrupted our conversation. Three burly police officers walked through the door and immediately took us to separate rooms to hear our versions of what had happened.

Afterward, we reconvened in the living room. The officer in charge said, "Mr. Sebastian, I understand from our discussion that you called to turn yourself in for almost losing control. Instead, I want to commend you for calling us. Very few people recognize their limits and call for help. You need to know that you were perfectly within your right to restrain your daughter. We are not going to arrest anyone today. At least your Dad had the restraint to stop and call for help," the officer said to Elizabeth. "I suggest you listen to your parents and stay out of trouble."

"I will," she answered demurely.

For a brief time, we had a reprieve from the battle of wills that sparked continual conflict and robbed us of our peace. I wish I could say that we lived happily ever after. Things improved for a few weeks yet, before long, we were back in the same cycle of anger and disrespect.

Hardened Hearts

As parents we strive to protect our children. In fact, since Elizabeth was our first child, I read every parenting book I could get my hands on from her earliest days. We tried to insulate her from every danger—real or imaginary—that could harm her. When she entered the teenage years, she increased her level of risk. We worried about her apparent disregard for the long-term repercussions of her actions and decisions.

Our response to Elizabeth's apparent reckless abandon was to trace the line in the sand again and again. She ignored our ultimatums and insisted on doing things her way. During this difficult time, I wished that I could gain access to her mind in order to push the buttons that would cause her to make the right decisions. That was impossible for me to do, yet I allowed her to 'push my buttons.'

We were locked in a destructive pattern with increased anger and frustration on both sides. Fear gripped my stomach every time I thought about where Elizabeth seemed to be heading. When did she become this sullen stranger who ignored everything we told her? The more her Dad and I tried to warn her about possible dangers ahead, the faster she sped in that direction.

Looking back, I'm reminded of the parable of the prodigal son in Luke 15. It seems Jesus could have been talking about our situation when he tells the story of the son who decided to go his own way. Even though we are not given many details, the older son's reactions reveal tension and anger that had been harbored.

In the culture of that day, the disrespect of the prodigal son was worthy of death by stoning. The young man's request for his share of the estate was in essence saying, "I wish my father were dead!" It also brought shame on the family, and most likely some property had to be sold in order to give the younger man his inheritance. The older son had good reasons to be outraged and indignant because what his brother was doing was wrong.

If I were to fill in the blanks, I can imagine that, from the older son's perspective, the story would go something like this . . .

"I can't believe my little brother would ask for his inheritance!" fumed the older son. His brother and his father had been fighting again. Well, it was more like the younger man yelling at the older one. "Frankly, I'm starting to lose respect for my father because he doesn't put my brother in his place. And as for my brother, I'm ready to disown him. Doesn't he see what he's doing to Dad? He's hurting him in ways I would never consider."

In spite of his anger, I'm sure he felt sad the night his brother left and fearful when he saw the sorrow in his father's eyes; he had never seen him look so vulnerable. "This is too hard on my father. This might be too much for him to take. It's all up to me now," he told himself. He quickly wiped the tears that sprang to his eyes. "I have to do everything I can to make up for what my brother has done," he resolved. Anger supplanted his vulnerable emotions of fear and uncertainty. He started to believe that he needed the strength of that anger to empower him to pick up the responsibilities his brother had dropped. As time passed, his anger hardened into deep-seated resentment.

UNRESOLVED ANGER ALIENATES

Unresolved anger can separate and alienate family members. When the younger son returned, his father threw a big party because he was so happy. The older son didn't share the same joy. In fact, he was extremely angry. He was the 'good' son who did everything he was supposed to do. He looked good on the outside, but unfortunately, bitterness and resentment toward his younger brother simmered under the surface. He hardened his heart and didn't want to even acknowledge he had a brother. Due to his anger which had festered, he went overboard in his martyr-like complex and work ethic. When he first heard the music, I imagine he headed home to see what the commotion was about.

"What's going on?" he shouted across the field to one of the young servants.

"We're having the party your father planned during the time your brother was gone. Your brother came home today so we are celebrating," the servant answered with trepidation.

"I always thought that the party planning was just a way for my father to feel better," he thought bitterly. "Of course, I also never dreamed my so-called 'brother' would ever actually come back. He has some nerve!"

"Aren't you going to come join the celebration?" the servant asked. "Your father has been asking about you."

"If my father asks again, just tell him I don't plan to come in," he said angrily.

A few minutes later, the father came out. He welcomed this chance to share his heart of love toward his older son who had become distant and cold. He stood next to him and prayed for wisdom to know how to comfort, encourage, and teach him.

"Why don't you come in and join the party, son," he said kindly.

"You know that I've been working like a slave all my life," the son said, giving vent to his pent up anger. "I gave up my own pursuits to make up for what your son did. I never got out of line. I've followed all of your rules and done everything you commanded me to do, but you've never thrown me a party. You never even spared a scrawny goat for a party for my friends, yet you've slaughtered the fattened calf for the son who blew it! He spent your money on prostitutes! Now this son of yours decides to come back after wasting everything, and you act like all is forgiven. You throw him this big party with steaks on the barbecue while I get nothing! I just don't get it!"

"Son, you don't understand," the father replied. "You're with me all the time, and everything belongs to you. No one can take that away from you. But this is a joyous time, and we had to celebrate. Your brother was lost and now is found. I thought he was dead, but he is alive!"

Controlled by Anger

During this difficult season with Elizabeth, I must confess that I became more like the angry older brother than the gracious father. I had made every effort to be the 'perfect' parent and do everything the right way. As Elizabeth headed in the wrong direction and insisted on her own way, I tried even harder to control the situation. When that didn't work, I turned my anger inward and eventually lost my illusion of control. The reality is that we cannot control others. Yet I found myself at times unable even to control myself. Certain triggers would set off my latent anger, and I would explode.

I began to dread my interactions with Elizabeth. I never knew if I was going to be the brunt of her anger, so I used anger as my defensive weapon. What resulted was a continual battle of wills—that I felt like I lost most of the time. I was most angry with myself for not being the perfect parent. The harder I tried, the more I failed.

In retrospect, it seems like our situation could have been solved so easily. Yet while we were in the middle of it, I was at a loss for what to do next because my anger dictated every move. Just like the older brother, I was outraged at my daughter's actions and felt justified in harboring resentment toward her because she was making wrong decisions. Unfortunately, this set up a destructive cycle of shouting matches followed by tears on both sides.

There is a better way. A hope perspective changed my outlook. When I'm angry now, I don't seek to understand every detail because I am too close to the problems. Instead, I step back and examine what I believe about the current situation. That's when I can see how God has been working. He is faithful and will continue to accomplish His purposes in my life and in the lives of those I love.

Looking back on it now, I can see clearly that we had engaged in a losing battle. I was angry and didn't even want to admit it. I wish I had taken steps to deal with the anger and re-establish the peace in our home.

Steps to Handling Anger

1 Admit you are angry. I called it a lot of other things such as frustration, annoyance, or irritation, but I was mad. Anger is a neutral emotion that we all can feel when we see injustice or when we feel hurt. Paul writes: "When angry, do not sin; do not ever let your wrath (your exasperation, your fury or indignation) last until the sun goes down. Leave no [such] room or foot-

hold for the devil [give no opportunity to him]" (Ephesians 4:26-27 Amplified). This scripture admonishes us to resolve quickly the issues that result from our anger. The verse does not say that we should never get angry. Instead, it acknowledges what to do when we become angry. We need to deal promptly with our anger so we don't give the enemy an opportunity to use it as a weapon against us. Unresolved anger hardens into deep-rooted bitterness that hinders relationships. We harden our hearts and can ignore our shortcomings while we point out the weaknesses of others.

2 Explore motives behind your anger. What happened to get you ticked off? Do you remember a time before in your life when you felt this anger before? Anger is an emotion that can arise when we feel vulnerable. It can feel 'safer' to stay mad rather than acknowledge the reasons behind it. I was afraid of what people would think. I was afraid I had failed as a parent. I was afraid Elizabeth would get hurt or lose her life. We may believe that the anger is making us strong or helping us to do something. James 1:19-20 says, "My dear brothers and sisters, take note of this: Everyone should be quick to listen, slow to speak and slow to become angry, because

human anger does not produce the righteousness of God." I felt like my anger was helping me be strong enough to show 'tough love.' Instead, the angry words we exchanged created roadblocks that kept us from moving forward. I became skeptical and suspicious of everything Elizabeth did. Instead of looking for the best in her, I expected the worst. Strangely enough, that's exactly what I got.

3 Figure out whom you are angry with. I felt very justified in my anger toward Elizabeth. What was not quite so apparent was the anger I had toward myself. I felt like it was my fault that we were going through this crisis. At times, I was angry with my husband as well, because I felt like he would give in to Elizabeth when I was trying to make a stand. Other times, I was the one who would give in. Also, I was angry at God for not answering our prayers for her.

4 Confess your anger. Ask Jesus to forgive you for holding on to your anger and acting out accordingly. Give the Lord the chance to share His perspective about the situation. He will give you His truth. Your heart will begin to soften toward the person with whom you were angry. You will also connect on a deeper level as you forgive them.

5 Release your anger. Be willing to face the fear and uncertainty that may be hiding underneath the anger. If you are willing to let the Lord be your defense rather than holding on to the anger, He will replace it with His truth. You can be at perfect peace as you begin to think like He does. 2 Thessalonians 3:16 says, "Now may the Lord of peace Himself give you peace at all times and in every way." So let it go, even if your child hasn't changed. Once we let go of our need to be in charge, we can watch the Lord work in the lives of our children while we enjoy His peace.

The father in the parable of the lost son approached both sons with grace. He met them right where they were. His focus was on building strong relationships rather than simply correcting their bad behavior. That's what I want for my family, and it has to start with me. As I've released my anger to the Lord, He has been faithful to give me His perspective. His viewpoint makes a difference and changes me from the inside out. God's perspective fills me with hope for today and for future generations. He restores balance and brings good from every circumstance.

Hope Tools

Here are three suggestions from Proverbs on ways to defuse anger in your interactions with your child:

1 Practice the art of a soft caring response. Proverbs 15:1 (MSG) says, "A gentle response defuses anger, but a sharp tongue kindles a temper-fire."

2 Give yourself a 'time-out' if you feel like you're losing control. Resume the conversation once you've calmed down. Proverbs 15:18 (MSG) says, "Hot tempers start fights; a calm, cool spirit keeps the peace."

3 Prepare and practice a neutral answer when you are challenged. Proverbs 19:11 (MSG) says, "Smart people know how to hold their tongue; their grandeur is to forgive and forget."

Write down other tips that have helped you minimize the tempers that can flare up when dealing with a rebellious child.

Prayer

Lord, forgive me for not handling my anger according to Your plan. I have harbored anger at _____, at myself, and even at You. I confess that anger to You. Thank You for your perspective which shows me that anger only separates me from those I love the most. I release the anger and ask You to replace it with peace and hope. From this day forward, help me make sure that by the end of each day I have dealt with any anger issues so that I do not sin (Ephesians 4:26).

Thank You for Your unchanging love toward me even when I have acted in ways that did not show Your love toward _____. Thank You for giving me words of hope and love for my child. By Your grace, these life-giving words will always fill my mouth and will continue to bless future generations (Isaiah 59:21).

I thank You for working in _____'s life and for following her/him with Your grace and mercy (Psalm 23:6). As Your Spirit lovingly guides _____ into a place of freedom (2 Corinthians 3:16), I look forward to our times together. We will not stay stuck in the past, yet we will learn the lessons we need to in order to move to the bright future You have planned for us.

In Jesus' name, Amen.

Hope Expressions

"As for me, this is my covenant with them," says the LORD. "My Spirit, who is on you, will not depart from you, and my words that I have put in your mouth will always be on your lips, on the lips of your children and on the lips of their descendants—from this time on and forever," says the LORD.

Isaiah 59:21

Caution:
Road Under Construction

All morning I felt a growing sense of impending doom. I kept reviewing my last conversation with Elizabeth—if you could call it that. It was actually more of a shouting match. It was getting harder and harder to get her up for school. None of the normal ways of waking her worked. This morning was no different. I yelled at her repeatedly. She finally got up but was sullen and angry. We fought the whole way to school.

"I hate you, Mom. I hate this stupid school. I hate my life!" she yelled at me.

"This is your fault, you know. You are the one who wanted to go to public school instead of working with your tutor, so now make the best of it!" I yelled back.

She slammed the car door and slowly walked over to a group of kids. She said something to them, and they all looked in my direction and laughed. They looked pretty rough around the edges. "I guess I better see if I can find out more about these kids she's hanging out with," I thought as I slowly drove away.

My heart sank as I thought about how far she was straying from the way we had raised her. On the way to work, I mulled over the decisions that brought us to this place. Elizabeth had been privately tutored for the last two years due to her learning disabilities. She made great progress, loved her tutor, and blossomed in this nurturing environment where she could learn without undue external pressure. All seemed fine on the surface, yet underneath Elizabeth longed to experience the things she thought she was missing. She wanted to attend public high school, and we agreed to let her go. Now, my heart was heavy with worry and guilt about the direction she was headed and the friends she was choosing.

I walked into my office and sat down at my desk. Mentally, I tried to set aside the issues with Elizabeth so I could concentrate on work. Recently I had been promoted to a new department and knew how important it was to make a good first impression. Not long after I began working, the phone rang. It was Elizabeth's school.

"I need to speak to Elizabeth Sebastian's mother."

"Speaking," I replied.

"You need to come to the school immediately to pick up your daughter. She's being suspended for vandalizing the girls' bathroom," said the dispassionate voice on the other end of the line.

"But I'm at work right now," I answered in a panic.

"Well, if you come now you can take her, and we won't have to call the authorities. It's up to you."

"I'll see what I can do," I replied.

"Okay, ma'am. The assistant principal wants to talk to you when you get here." Clunk—dial tone.

I checked my calendar and headed to my boss's office to let him know I would need to leave. Since I was new in the department, I had not shared my personal problems with anyone. I knocked on my boss's door. He looked up and motioned me to come in.

"I need to leave due to some problems at my daughter's school."

"Is there anything I can do?" he replied.

"Not really. I just received a call telling me that she's involved in some type of school property vandalism." My voice caught in my throat as I attempted to hold back the tears.

"Close the door for a moment," he said.

As I moved toward the door to close it, I struggled to keep my composure. This was not very professional.

This is no way to start a new position, I chided myself. My throat hurt as I swallowed hard in a feeble attempt to hold back the tears.

"I don't share this with too many people, Karen," my boss continued. "Our son has been in and out of rehab for several years. I know what you're going through. Go ahead and take care of this, and don't worry about work right now."

"Thank you so much," I answered. I felt relieved to know that my new boss understood what I was going through. At the same time, I dreaded what was ahead.

Emotional Rollercoaster

On the way to the school, my emotions flashed hot and cold. I went from extreme anger where I pounded the steering wheel to overwhelming sadness as I blamed myself for what was happening in our family.

As I pulled into the school parking lot, I glanced at my reflection in the rear view mirror. *Pull yourself together, Karen,* I told myself as I tried to wipe away the eye makeup smeared on my face. It was no use. I only made it worse. Each step I climbed to the entrance of the school filled me with greater despair and dread. How could our daughter be in this kind of trouble?

I found my way to the assistant principal's office and sat there until a very officious young man walked in and introduced himself. He sat down at his desk and stared at me for a few seconds. The serious look on his face revealed his anger.

"Your daughter is in a lot of trouble, Mrs. Sebastian," he stated firmly.

"What exactly happened?" I queried.

"We're still checking into the whole situation, but your daughter and another student made a complete mess out of the girls' restroom."

"That's what I was told over the phone. What do we do next?" I asked timidly.

"Well, ma'am, it's not so much what *we* will do, it's what *you* will do. I assume you are a single mom. This happens a lot with kids who don't have a strong father figure," he continued.

"I don't know how you got that impression. My husband and I care a lot for our daughter."

"She's trouble. I can spot the ones who are going to cause trouble. I can tell by the way they look at me. And I can tell you another thing, the kids she is hanging around are also trouble."

"What do you recommend that we do?"

"Well, obviously there's no consistent discipline at home," he said matter-of-factly. "You need to get a handle on this situation right now. If she continues this way, she will probably end up in jail."

Harsh Judgments

With each harsh judgment coming from this man's mouth, my heart sank into deeper despair. He was confirming my greatest fears for our daughter. I wanted to defend her, but he seemed so sure of what he was saying that I remained silent. Worse yet, he seemed to be saying that this situation was our fault for our lack of consistent discipline. Of course, he knew nothing about us and was jumping to many false conclusions. But I chose to believe these lies because I was insecure about my parenting abilities. He concluded the conversation by stating that our daughter was suspended from school and I needed to take her home.

As I waited outside the school for Elizabeth, hot tears welled up in my eyes and I could no longer contain them. I felt humiliated and angry. When I saw Elizabeth walking toward me, I was relieved that she seemed subdued. "Good!" I thought. "This time she's going to listen to what I have to say."

A wave of anger washed over me, covering the fear and embarrassment I felt. I wanted Elizabeth to know how unhappy I was about the events of the day. The minute she got into the car, I started yelling. "What is wrong with you? Do you have any idea how much trouble you've caused me? I just got a new job and I'm not making a good impression by having to leave because of what you've done," I exclaimed emphatically. I failed to share how the Lord had given me favor with my new boss because of it.

"Mom, listen to me. I didn't do anything. The bathroom was trashed when I walked in," she replied.

I was now on a roll and completely blew past her comment. "You are headed down a dangerous path, young lady. You better watch who you hang out with because if you are with the wrong kids, you will get in trouble too," I persisted.

"Mom, I didn't do anything. Why don't you believe me?" she went on. A few tears slipped down her cheeks, which she quickly wiped away.

The rest of the way home, I continued to rant about all the things she was doing wrong. For once, she remained silent, which at the time I thought was a good thing. When we got home, she slammed the car door behind her and ran inside. By the time I walked into the house, the rhythm of heavy metal music was vibrating from her bedroom.

I didn't believe her because recently I had caught her in several lies. I sided with her enemies. As a result, I pushed her toward the very things that I feared. She was expelled from school and her hard responses impressed the ringleader of the new group. They soon became close friends. I missed a golden opportunity to communicate with my daughter.

The facts of the situation kept me from making a heart connection with her at that vulnerable moment. I accused her instead of asking questions that would have stimulated further communication. I agreed with her enemies and stated the facts rather than the truth.

Facts condemn—the truth sets us free. The facts said that our daughter was messing up. The truth was that she could turn around at any point in time. The fact was she was hanging out with a rough crowd. The truth from a love vantage declared that she is a strong leader who is not that easily influenced by others.

WORDS ARE POWERFUL

Our words are powerful. Angry words and threats remain in the atmosphere even after we apologize for them. More importantly, when angry words of condemnation are spoken over a child, they reinforce their sense of inadequacy and failure. In Deuteronomy 30:19 the Bible says, "I have set before you life and death, blessing and cursing; therefore choose life, that both you and your descendants may live." We often think of cursing as a slip of the tongue when we say certain choice words. It is much more than that. It can take the form of belittling and putting someone down. This type of angry tirade from a parent or teacher can cause great damage. My word patterns were intended to keep my daughter in line. Instead, the ultimatums made it hard for me to go back to what needed to be done. My words set our family on a road that was full of land mines and pitfalls. My pride kept me from going back on what I said was going to do.

Hope Tools

LISTEN

I look back and see many missed opportunities to speak the truth in love. Our words can eliminate hope no matter how accurate our facts may be about any given situation. My own pain caused me to miss the chance to hear her side of the story—to gain her perspective.

Listen twice as much as you speak. Listening is an art that must be cultivated. Start by asking open-ended questions that start with When-Where-Why-How rather than questions that require a 'yes' or 'no' answer. Your goal is to get them talking so you can gain insight into what is happening in their lives. At first, the pause after the questions may seem somewhat uncomfortable. Fight the urge to fill the silence; give them a chance to answer. Listening is more important.

Increase eye contact. Research shows that while our words are important, our tone of voice, facial expressions and body language come through as well. If they do not match, we will believe what we see. Show your interest by tuning in with your body language. Pay full attention to the feelings behind what is said.

Say what you mean and mean what you say. There are two communication extremes: The first is to bark out orders and the second is to hint at what you would like others to do. Neither is effective. The first one backfires because you are not respecting the other person, and they learn to give orders back. Yet when you hint at what you want others to do, they are confused and frustrated because they can't read your mind. Communication clears up when there are no hidden agendas. Don't wait until you're frustrated before you blurt out what you really want to say.

Take their body language in stride. One of the land mines in my communication with Elizabeth was my over-reaction to her body language. I would hit the roof when she acted like she was ignoring me or rolled her eyes. Keep repeating the main message in different ways until you are sure that it got through.

Establish clear expectations. Keep your sentences short and clear when giving instructions. Establish clear expectations by providing definite choices. Get to your point quickly and increase buy-in by giving reasons why you need something. Avoid qualifiers such as "very" and "really." The use of absolutes such as "always" and "never" can also beg for a heated discussion about the exceptions.

Nurture the relationship. Open the communication channels when possible. Look for opportunities to speak encouraging words. If your child has gotten into trouble recently, prepare yourself to talk to him or her about your love and support. This conversation can reveal what is going on under the surface. What are the real issues? What does your child feel? What can they learn from this experience? Wait for a window of opportunity. When it opens, speak the truth in love.

FACT VS. TRUTH

Find a quiet place to think about your last confrontation with your child. On a sheet of paper, write down the facts about the situation. Take a moment to pray for the loving heart of our Heavenly Father. Next to each fact, write the truth about the problem.

Example:

Facts	Truth
This is a difficult time.	We will make it through this hard time with the help of God.
My child is out of control.	My child is making wrong choices but the road home is closer than she/he realizes.
The future seems dismal because of all the wrong choices my child is making.	This is a challenging time because of wrong choices my child is making, yet God will bring good and accomplish His purpose as she/he turns to Him.
I can't take this any longer.	I have the strength that I need to make it through this difficult time.

PRAYER

Father, I want to worship You in spirit and in truth (John 4:24 KJV). Forgive me for my harsh words toward _____. Show me how to replace them with words of blessing and truth. I long to speak the truth in love (Ephesians 4:15). As we come into the knowledge of Your truth, I believe we will be set free. I trust You to guide her/him into all truth (John 16:13).

Father, I invite You in to our difficult situation and ask You to bring healing to our relationship. Forgive me for coming down too hard on _____ just for the sake of being right. Do not allow this to crush her/his spirit (Col. 3:21 MSG). Restore trust and rebuild our relationship. I thank You for speaking to her/him and revealing that there is no fear in love (1 John 4:18). Open _____'s eyes to Your power to overcome all obstacles and guide her/him to a place of confidence in You. Keep _____ from falling or stumbling as she/he puts her/his faith in You (Jude 1:24).

Start with me. Please give me the grace to show _____ Your steadfast and unchanging love. Help me to establish new communication patterns of trust and love in our home. Change the atmosphere and make our home a place of peace, love, and joy. I need Your help, Father, to face my fears regarding _____. I have lost hope for any positive outcome in this situation. You are the restorer of hope and the giver of all good things. I ask You to restore the hope and joy we have lost (Proverbs 10:28).

In Jesus' name, Amen.

HOPE EXPRESSIONS

I'll take the hand of those who don't know the way, who can't see where they're going. I'll be a personal guide to them, directing them through unknown country. I'll be right there to show them what roads to take, make sure they don't fall into the ditch. These are the things I'll be doing for them—sticking with them, not leaving them for a minute.

Isaiah 42:16 ~ The Message

Avoiding Danger Ahead

No words can fully describe the devastation I felt when I first realized that our daughter was using drugs. I ran into the bathroom and vomited. I had caught her in one lie after another. Her behavior had become so erratic that we could not predict what she would do next.

A heaviness grew and lurked in the pit of my stomach—a combination of fear, dread, anger, frustration, and hurt. Those who have a rebellious child are probably familiar with the feeling I am trying to describe. It ranges from a vague apprehension to a hard knot in your stomach. While you may stop thinking about it for a short while, a simple trigger such as a ringing phone can cause it to rush back with an overwhelming sense of dread.

When I first suspected that our daughter was headed for trouble, a sense of uneasiness crept in. Even though something deep inside told me there were danger signs, I ignored them, hoping they would go away. I somehow managed to set my concerns aside for short periods. In retrospect, I realize I took an ostrich approach by putting my head in the sand. Maybe . . . just maybe . . . I would wake up one day and my daughter would have outgrown this 'stage.'

That wishful thinking came crashing down the morning I walked into our daughter's empty bedroom. The window was cracked open and the screen had been pushed out. She had crawled out the window some time during the night. All my fears hit me in the face and my faith was shaken to the core.

Frantically, I started calling her friends. They seemed surprised that I would call them and said they hadn't spent much time with her lately. A sick feeling permeated my stomach. I had been right! I should have listened to my intuition. Something had been telling me that there was more going on under the surface, but I had let things slide. Lately, I had suspected that Elizabeth was lying about where she was going, and she was increasingly hostile. I felt desperate to find her now and get things back to normal. I called every number I could find in the papers littering her room, and finally we found out where she was.

I called the police and told them our daughter had run away. "What would you do if this was your daughter?" I asked.

The voice on the other end of the line hesitated for a moment. "Well, ma'am, we usually don't get asked that question," the officer replied. "You said that you know where she is, right?"

We knew she was in a safe place but wanted to teach her a lesson.

"What I would suggest is that you let us send out two of our toughest guys. They will really scare her. That way she won't want to do it again. She'll know you mean business. We'll call you so you can pick her up at the juvenile detention center."

I hesitated. I remembered talking to other parents who found good results from practicing what they called 'tough love.' After talking it over with my husband, we decided it was worth a try. We were desperate. When the police called to say they had her in custody, we immediately got in the car and headed to the detention center.

My husband drove quickly, lost in his thoughts. I wanted to talk about my conflicting emotions, but the look on his face told me this was not a good time. After twenty years of marriage, I knew him well. Up to this point, we had faced our life crises together. This time it was different. An unspoken barrier hung between us. In our frustration with our daughter's behavior, we often ended up saying angry words to each other.

"Why do you let her talk to you that way?" my husband would say to me.

"Well, it would help if you would stop giving in to her and choosing her over me," I would counter.

We would go back and forth in a never-ending blame game. At a time that we most needed each other, we were fighting. It was a battle that no one would win.

As we drove along, I pictured the happy ending to our desperate strategy. It would unfold just like a scene from a 30-minute television drama. Once we got to the detention center and told the policeman our daughter's name, he would gruffly say, "Follow me. We have her in our interrogation room."

I would slowly open the door of the stark room where Elizabeth waited. She would look up at me with an expression of incredulous relief. Then she would run into my outstretched arms. (Of course, this would be in slow motion with flowing, tear-producing music.) We would hug and she would start crying, "Mom, I'm so sorry. I promise I will never, ever do that again."

My reply would be, "That's okay, honey. You know we only did this because we love you."

"I know Mom. I love you too," she would answer. (The music would crescendo as we stared into each other's eyes.) Elizabeth would wipe away a tear. We would walk back to the car arm in arm. (Picture fades.) Our problems would be solved. End of story.

An abrupt stop at a signal brought me back to reality. One turn later, we arrived in front of juvenile hall. I didn't want to wait until we could find a parking space, so my husband let me out in front. My heart pounded as I walked into the building. Immediately, I knew something was wrong with this scenario. The woman at the front desk glanced up briefly when I told her I was there to pick up my daughter. "First time, huh?" she asked. She looked back down at her computer screen and commented, "Boy, you sure got here fast. After the first or second time, most parents leave them here for a while—either trying to teach them a lesson or enjoying a brief moment of peace. Anyway, take a seat. It'll be a while since we haven't even started processing the paper work."

I bit my lip to keep from telling her our whole story—how we really were good parents and we were in the ministry and this should not be happening to us. I shuffled over to the magazine rack, picking up an outdated magazine before sitting next to my husband who had come in.

I pretended to read as I looked at others in the waiting area. An older lady caught my attention. She wore a stern expression on her tired face. A female police officer brought out a teenage girl. She looked younger than our daughter yet had the hardened look of a gang member. As our gaze met, the hateful look in her eyes startled me. The older woman walked over to the front desk, signed some papers, and angrily stomped toward the door without even looking back. The girl glared defiantly at her. The woman turned and yelled, "This better be the last time you do this! Do you hear me? Your parents already gave up on you and I'm pretty close. What's the matter with you?" As the door closed behind them, I heard their angry voices begin a heated argument. The lady at the desk just shook her head and went back to her work.

The door opened again, and this time it was the same lady officer with our daughter. My husband and I both stood up. I walked over to Elizabeth and hugged her. "How are you, sweetie?"

She stiffened against my hug. "What do you care? Did you call the cops on me? I know it was you. I hate you."

My heart felt like someone had ripped it out and plunged it into a bucket of ice water. Tears coursed down my cheeks. I was speechless. I had not prepared for this kind of scenario.

"You weren't so tough a little while ago were you, young lady?" the officer asked sarcastically. "You better be grateful you have parents who care enough to come and pick you up." Elizabeth just glared at both of us.

Frankly, I don't remember what happened next or what we said on the ride home. The whole experience was surreal. We were thrust into a world we had only read about in newspapers or seen in movies. How could this be happening to us? I wish I could tell you that the solution to this dark time came in a neat package within the time frame of a 30-minute show.

The resolution did not happen quickly. In fact, this experience hardened Elizabeth and seemed to push her in the wrong direction. When the 'tough love' approach didn't work, desperation became a familiar feeling. We went to anger management classes and family counseling. No matter what we did, things just got worse. Over the next five years, her behavior grew progressively more dangerous. She dropped out of school, experimented with drugs, dabbled in the occult, got involved in a gang, and spun further and further out of control.

Desperate Times

Elizabeth was in the fourth grade the first time she went into a rage. I don't even know what sparked it. She ran into her bedroom and threw everything on the ground. When I walked in to see what was going on, she started screaming, "I hate you! I hate you!" I was devastated and cried for days.

We couldn't afford to pay for Christian counseling, but we searched for answers through every means available. A doctor diagnosed her with Attention Deficit Hyperactive Disorder. She would be so frustrated when she came home from school that she would take her anger out on all of us. We took her to tutors and put her in special classes. I was very concerned about the labels her teachers and counselors put on her, but I didn't know what to do. I felt desperate and hopeless.

An incident recorded in the Gospel of Mark, chapter 9, shows a father with that same desperation. He had reached the end of his rope in dealing with his son's dangerous condition. He was afraid his son would die. He didn't know where else to turn. To make matters worse, Jesus wasn't there when he went to find Him, and the disciples were unable to help. When Jesus came down the mountain, the man ran to Him to complain that the disciples had failed.

"How long has this been going on?" asked Jesus.

"Since he was a little boy. He's fallen many times into the fire and the river. I'm afraid he will die. If you can do anything, do it. Have a heart. You've helped others so please help us," he cried desperately.

"If? There are no 'ifs' among believers. Anything can happen!" replied Jesus.

Standing right there in the presence of the Lord Jesus Christ, this father's faith expanded. All skepticism dropped away and he cried out, "Then I believe. Help me with my doubts!"

Hope came alive as this father laid aside his efforts to bring about change and instead set his focus on Jesus. Contrast this with the religious leaders who were arguing and even the disciples who were seeking a formula to set the boy free. They attempted what had worked in the past, and Jesus rebuked them as unbelieving. Rather than trusting God, they had put their faith in human efforts and systems.

Jesus took authority over the evil spirit and restored the boy to health and life. This dad learned that it was not enough just to know about the Master and what He can do. It's not enough to do what you've done in the past. That's where I found myself as I struggled with Elizabeth's behavior. Like the father in his desperation, I focused on my child's problem behavior and my own fears. I was desperate to find a solution. I was filled with doubt and unbelief. Don't make the same mistake.

Focus on Jesus and what He can accomplish when nothing else works. Bring your doubts out in the open and face them. What do you believe about the situation you currently face with your prodigal? Our situation became so dire that I eventually threw my hands up in despair. It was at that lowest point that I turned to the Lord for His perspective of hope. Jesus always meets us exactly where we are, and miracles happen when we believe in Him.

Hope Tools

WAYS TO COPE

One of the hardest things when dealing with dangerous behavior is to cope with feelings of despair and unbelief. Here are four ways you can change to a faith outlook and regain a sense of purpose.

Control what you can; let go of the rest. I panicked when I realized Elizabeth had run away. I completely overreacted and called the police. The measures I took were drastic and out of proportion. In retrospect, that was partly because I felt like I had lost control. When we argued, I would threaten to do drastic things but never follow through. So this time, I took drastic action hoping for change and a quick resolution to our problems. A better choice would have been to walk in peace knowing that God is in control. Jesus says to us,

"Do not let your hearts be troubled. Trust in God; trust also in me (John 14:1)."

Overcome fear. Take a good look at what you fear the most. In my case, I was afraid of the future because of the poor decisions my daughter made on a consistent basis. I was afraid she would die. I was afraid I had failed as a parent. I felt unsure about what to do next. My way of coping was to push the painful feelings down. I remember crying and asking the Lord to take all my emotions away. As a result, I felt numb most of the time except when I exploded in anger. There is a better way. Acknowledge and face what you most fear, and ask God to reveal His love. Once you face it, ask the Lord for His perspective, knowing that as you experience His love and grace, fear will vanish. "There is no fear in love. But perfect love drives out fear, because fear has to do with punishment. The one who fears is not made perfect in love (I John 4:18)."

Prepare your heart to listen. You can feel overwhelmed and helpless when your child keeps making wrong choices. I had no idea what to do when I realized that Elizabeth had run away. I wish I had gotten still and asked for God's direction. I wish I had asked more questions to find out where she was coming from. In our case, calling the police to take her to the detention center was overreacting. She hardened her heart and continued running in the wrong direction. I wish I had listened more and worked on our relationship rather than focusing on the external behavior. No matter what happens in our lives, God is greater and wants to direct our steps. He says, "Be still, and know that I am God; I will be exalted among the nations, I will be exalted in the earth (Psalm 46:10)."

Expect a positive outcome. My mental scenarios did not end well. The more I talked to others in similar circumstances with rebellious children, the more desperate I became. Filled with unbelief, I doubted that God could change our situation because nothing seemed to work. I was in a prison cell, captive to my unfulfilled expectations and disappointments. Invite the Lord into that place. Do not hide or pretend that you are fine. He is not surprised at what you are feeling or disappointed by what you have done. Focus on your relationship with Him. He wants to break you out of the hopelessness you now feel. He wants to restore relationships and give you a testimony. He is present when you feel defeated and stressed. He knows exactly what you are feeling and will meet you exactly where you are. Trust that God is working deeply and gently from the inside out.

"God can do anything, you know—far more than you could ever imagine or guess or request in your wildest dreams! He does it not by pushing us around but by working within us, his Spirit deeply and gently within us (Ephesians 3:20 MSG)."

PRAYER

I thank You, Heavenly Father, that You are always with me. I also thank You that You are with _____. Thank You for taking my hand because I can't see where we are going. It brings me peace to know that You are guiding me and directing my steps through unknown country. Thank You for sticking with us and not leaving us (Isaiah 42:16 MSG).

I confess my fears to You and thank You for replacing that fear with Your love. You give me the strength and power to make sound decisions about _____ (2 Timothy 1:7). Show me areas where I have believed lies about myself as a parent and have doubted the fact that You are a good God. I trust You to work in these areas and in the hearts of those I love. I put my trust in You to accomplish Your plan for my family (Isaiah 8:7).

I quiet myself before You and ask for grace to listen—really listen—to _____ (Matthew 11:15 MSG). I recognize that I need Your help to move forward. I release all my hopes and expectations to You. I acknowledge that Your plans are better than mine. I choose to lift my eyes from the ashes of my failure as a parent. I put _____ in Your capable hands. I trust that You will fulfill Your purposes for her/him because Your love endures forever and You will not abandon the work of Your hands (Psalms 138:8). I choose to seek You and rejoice in You. I know that those who trust in You will never be disappointed. Be magnified in our situation (Psalm 70:4).

Thank You for releasing _____ from her/his prison of hopelessness. You will restore and give us a double bonus of everything we have lost (Zechariah 9:12 MSG). I also accept the key to my hopeless prison cell from You, and I move forward to expect a good outcome.

In Jesus' name, Amen.

Hope Expressions

Now faith is being sure of what we hope for and certain of what we do not see.

Hebrews 11:1

Stopping at Rest Stops

After we moved to Texas, we made several trips across the country to visit family and friends in California. One stretch of road between Abilene and El Paso seems to go on forever. In that deserted landscape, it is a welcome relief to see signs indicating a rest stop is coming shortly. In the middle of our difficult time with Elizabeth, it felt as if we were on an endless trip across the desert with no rest areas in sight. There were rest areas, however; we were just too preoccupied to use them. We were so determined to get through our problems that we didn't take time to take care of ourselves.

TAKE CARE OF YOURSELF FIRST

Each time you board a plane, you hear a speech about the oxygen mask that will drop down in case of an emergency. "If you are traveling with a child, put your mask on first and then help your child." It's easy to neglect your own health and get pulled into a desperate mindset. Remember to take care of yourself as you are caring for everyone else.

During this difficult time, I began to show symptoms that I was not getting enough 'hope' oxygen. Frazzled and worn out, I exploded in anger over minor setbacks. I had lost all hope that our daughter would ever turn around. Proverbs 13:12 says, "Hope deferred makes the heart sick." I had a sick feeling in the pit of my stomach every time I thought about her. I also began experiencing other physical symptoms such as joint pain. One morning I woke up and noticed a strange rash across my nose and cheeks. It was in the shape of a butterfly. I went to the doctor and was diagnosed with lupus.

As I got in my car after the appointment, I put my head on the steering wheel and started sobbing. I felt so weak. Something had to change. As I looked at all my options, I realized the one thing that I could change was my attitude. I had relinquished my sense of well-being to my daughter. I cheered up when she was doing well and was devastated by every step she took in the wrong direction. My efforts to control Elizabeth were not working. I determined to regain control of my own attitude toward the situation.

I cried out to the Lord asking Him to carry this weight. I felt powerless. "Lord, I can't do this anymore," I cried. "I need You to restore my hope. We can't keep going like this. I trust You with Elizabeth. I'm going to let You carry this weight the rest of the way during this journey because I can't do it anymore. And one more thing—I'm leaving the timing up to You."

A Drink of Living Water

I was desperate for a refreshing drink of water just like the Samaritan woman in John 4. She went to the public well for water during the hottest part of the day in order to avoid the gossiping neighbors. She would rather not go at all, but had no other choices. Because she had made horrible mistakes in her relationships, she suffered the shame of being an outcast. Nevertheless, she was a survivor who had figured out the best way to make it through difficult times. As I read the scriptures, I can imagine what she was thinking as she went to get water.

Shielding her eyes as she walked up to the well, she saw a man sitting there. *I think he's a Jew so I'll be okay. They don't speak to women in public—especially to a Samaritan like me*, she thought. She avoided eye contact by keeping her head down, but as she pulled up her pot filled with water, He asked her for a drink. His accent confirmed that He was indeed Jewish.

"How come you, a Jew, are asking me, a Samaritan woman, for a drink?" she asked in a shocked voice. Not only was He talking to her, but He was even willing to drink from the vessel that she had to offer. She looked up briefly as she handed Him the water pot and saw kindness there that was unknown to her.

"If you knew the generosity of God and who I am, you would be asking me for a drink, and I would give you fresh, living water," was His reply.

This man was crazy because this was a well that Jacob dug. "Sir, you don't even have a bucket to draw with, and this well is deep," she said quickly.

"Everyone who drinks this water will get thirsty again and again. Anyone who drinks the water I give will never thirst—not ever. The water I give will be an artesian spring within, gushing fountains of endless life," He further explained.

"Sir, give me this water so I won't ever be thirsty, and I won't ever have to come back to this well again!" she exclaimed.

The story goes on to speak about her need to come to the Lord just as she was so that He could redeem the sins of the past. The Master knows all about our shortcomings and likes us to be open about them. He wants to give us an ongoing supply of living water. He provides us with everything we need during those long stretches of desert. Hope for the future comes from drinking deeply from the running spring of His living water.

Set Healthy Boundaries

The first change I made to begin taking better care of myself was to set realistic boundaries to protect the quality of life for the rest of the family. Elizabeth's needs were important, but not more important than the needs of everyone else. It was important to find a balance between cutting her off completely with the 'tough love' approach and smothering her with over-indulgent sympathy for the hard time she was having. Neither approach is healthy. The balance is somewhere in the middle and starts with the parent. Talk about the reason you are setting the boundaries and come to agreement. Make this a respectful dialogue with your child. Once you agree on the boundaries, talk about consequences. The best way to do this is to allow your child to suffer the consequences of their behavior instead of rescuing them.

One boundary that was effective during these turbulent times was the agreement between Elizabeth, her dad, and me that she would not get any tattoos until she turned eighteen. She agreed with the consequence that if she got a tattoo, we would not buy her a car. We did not handle all the boundaries as well as we did this one, but sticking to it reaped benefits later. She recently told me, "You know, Mom, at the time I hated your stance on the tattoos. But I was into so much stuff back then, I would probably be saving my money to remove a bunch of them now."

SHARE LAUGHTER

"One of these days this whole mess is going to be funny," my friend mentioned one day as we talked about our daughters.

"I don't think that will work for me right now," I mumbled. I was in such a dark place that I just felt numb.

"At least you can try to smile a little more," she replied. "I miss your smile."

I knew I was letting this situation with Elizabeth consume me. It wasn't the only challenge that we faced, but it was the most consuming. It filled every waking moment and even invaded my dreams. I needed a way of escape.

On my commute to work the next day, I made a conscious decision that I would become the most positive person that I knew. I wasn't sure what that looked like, and it seemed impossible at the time. I started with smiling—I mean making a conscious effort to smile even when I didn't feel like it.

Laughter is a very important hope tool. Of course, looking back, there are things that seem funny now that weren't funny at the time we were going through them. In the scheme of things, how significant is blue, purple, or green hair? I only wish that I had taken pictures. My sense of shame kept me from laughing.

When was the last time you had a good laugh—the kind that leaves you with your sides aching? You may be thinking, "Do you have any idea what I am going through? There is nothing funny about our situation." No doubt that is true if you are identifying with me. What I am talking about is the joy that comes from inside when you let go of shame regarding your child's behavior. Have you noticed that you can't stay mad when you laugh? As I developed a sense of humor about the situation with Elizabeth, a subtle shift took place in me. The more hope I felt, the more I could laugh. It's even more releasing to laugh with others who share our joy.

Strengthen other Relationships

Maintain a balance of life outside of the difficult situation with your child. Sustain relationships with supportive friends and family. This is a good time to seek out other activities and interests. Refrain from talking exclusively about the problems. It will give you a breather and a different perspective.

Maintain a Healthy Regime

It is critical to take care of yourself physically by eating right, exercising regularly, and sleeping a minimum of 8 hours. These habits will keep you strong physically and emotionally. Give yourself permission to rest. When you feel like your child is out of control, you can become obsessed with busyness just so you don't have to face the situation. A rest stop allows you to relax and recharge.

I am happy to report that my health improved once I made a shift from negativity to hope. The transformation was radical and affected not only my emotions, but my body as well. When I returned to the doctor a few months later, they no longer found the lupus symptoms.

Hope Tools

Rest Stops

A rest stop is any activity that allows you to get your mind off your problems long enough to gain perspective. It can be as simple as taking a deep breath and as involved as going for a weekend retreat. Regardless of what you choose—be consistent and regularly take these breaks. Take care of yourself first.

Examples:

Prayer

Time with friends

Reading

Taking a walk

Hobby

Taking a nap

Going for a drive

Laughing

PUT ON YOUR OXYGEN MASK FIRST

Make time for yourself. It's easy to neglect taking care of yourself when your family is in crisis. Just like the message on the airplane as you take off, grab that oxygen mask and bring it down to your face. Take a deep breath and then hand it to your child. This is not a selfish thing to do—it is survival. You need time to think, re-group, and recharge. It is important to take care of your own needs when going through tough times with a rebellious child. Engage in what you enjoy and get away from the problems long enough to gain perspective.

"Therefore with joy will you draw water from the wells of salvation (Isaiah 12:3)."

Avoid complaining. Negativity and hope cannot coexist. In the beginning years of our difficult time, I would share my problems with anyone who would listen. After these conversations, I would feel defeated and hopeless. Live each day without projecting doom and gloom. Take care of what you can and let go of the rest. "Do everything without complaining or arguing (Philippians 2:14)."

Set realistic expectations for yourself. Take off the pressure to be perfect and for those around you to be the same. We all can make mistakes, and that is okay as long as we learn from them. Be transparent about your struggles. If you fall in a certain area, get right back up and move ahead. Celebrate every step in the right direction. Seek to please God as you go through the challenging times. "We are not trying to please men but God, who tests our hearts (I Thessalonians 2:4)."

Keep track of your blessings. While you may be going through a tough time, thinking about your blessings balances out the pain. The other benefit of focusing on blessings is that you realize you have so much to be grateful for despite the difficulties of the moment. This perspective allows you to create an atmosphere of hope for the future as you find joy and grow stronger. "And be not grieved and depressed, for the joy of the Lord is your strength and stronghold (Nehemiah 8: 10)."

PRAYER

Thank You, Lord, for the strength of the three-fold strand of faith, hope, and love (I Corinthians 13:13) that connects me to Your life. I recognize my need to put on my oxygen mask first, and so I take the oxygen mask of prayer and invite You into my current situation with _____.

(Inhale then exhale slowly) I breathe in faith. There are times when I feel inadequate in this area, but I know You are the Author of my faith (Hebrews 12:2). I ask You to fill my spirit with a higher measure of faith to trust what You are doing in _____'s life even when I cannot see anything good happening.

(Inhale then exhale slowly) I take a deep breath of hope. I know that You are the only one who can make good come from our mistakes. I feel out of control and at a loss of what to do next. I admit that recently I have lost hope that there will be a change. Give me the gift of hope—a confident expectation that You are working in _____'s life even when I don't see it. I know You are the hope of glory (Colossians 1:27) and I ask You to flood her/his life with renewed hope that the road home is shorter than she/he thinks.

(Inhale then exhale slowly) I take a deep breath of Your love. You love us with an everlasting love (Jeremiah 31:3). This means You love us unconditionally just the way we are. I know You love _____ even more than I do and that I can trust You to take care of her/him. I trust You to show her/him how much You love and care for her/him. I know that as I begin to walk in hope, faith, and love toward _____, You will provide the same in her/his life.

I pray this in Jesus' powerful name, Amen.

HOPE EXPRESSIONS

I want a cabin in the woods. I'm desperate for a change from rage and stormy weather.
Psalm 55:7 ~ The Message

PREPARE THE WAY HOME

Getting Back in the Driver's Seat

"Mom, ple-e-e-ease leave the keys in the car so I can listen to music," pleaded Elizabeth.

"I won't be in the store long," I replied. "Why don't you come in with me?"

"It's so boring," she whined.

"Okay, but don't touch anything," I yelled back at her as I slammed the door.

In the past few months, my relationship with Elizabeth had eroded to the point that I didn't trust her even for a few minutes. I ran to the back of the store to get the bread and milk. The checkout line seemed to take forever as an unexplainable sense of dread overwhelmed me.

"I never should have left her in the car with the keys. What in the world was I thinking? How stupid can I be?" I berated myself.

My fears were confirmed as I came out of the store. Elizabeth had backed the car out of the parking spot. She turned too sharply and left a deep scratch on the passenger side of the car parked next to ours. I panicked when I saw what Elizabeth had done.

"Look what you've done now! Move, just move!" I screamed at her.

I got in the driver's seat and slammed the door. Putting my face in my hands, I fought back a wave of panic. I have replayed the next few seconds over and over in my mind, wishing I had made a more logical, sane decision. I put the car in reverse and drove away as fast as I could. I kept looking in the rear view mirror thinking that I would see flashing lights.

I ranted all the way home. I was completely out of control, alternating between shame and anger. I was angry at her and at myself, and terribly ashamed that I had fled the scene of the accident. It is difficult to talk about this, yet I share it because I know some of you can relate to being right on the edge of doing something you never thought you were capable of doing. It is a frightening place to be.

When we got home, Elizabeth ran to her room and slammed the door. I walked right past my husband without saying a word. Retreating to my bedroom in shame, I fell across the bed and sobbed. In the beginning, I even lied to my husband about the dented bumper because I felt so ashamed of what I had done. The issue finally came to light when an insurance company phoned, notifying me that someone had turned in my license plate number. Our insurance took care of the damages, and I took all the blame.

That is how Elizabeth's driving started. Even before she had her driver's license, she was ready to go. At this time, I threw my hands up in despair and let go of the steering wheel. The next five years were dark and hopeless as it felt like she was driving the entire family over a cliff.

Learning Empathy

The Bible is brutally honest about the weaknesses of the people in it. I think that's so we can be encouraged in our own struggles. I'm reminded of Peter, one of Jesus' disciples who was bold one minute and a coward the next. He was a rough fisherman who had spent the last three years with Jesus. Despite his rough edges, he loved his Master from the depths of his heart. When the religious leaders came to arrest Jesus in the Garden of Gethsemane, the other disciples asked, "Master, shall we fight?" Not Peter! Even before Jesus could answer, he came out swinging his sword and cut off the ear of one of the servants (Luke 22:49-51). Jesus quietly healed the ear and then surrendered to the temple guards without a struggle.

As the story unfolds, the guards led Jesus to the house of the chief priest. Most of the disciples ran away but Peter followed, albeit at a distance. He lurked in the shadows, waiting to see what would happen to his beloved teacher. Shivering against the cool breeze on that dark morning, Peter moved closer to the fire to dispel the coldness which he felt all the way to his core. One of the servant girls recognized him and said loudly, "Aren't you one of the followers of the Nazarene?"

The young maiden's words chilled him even further. "I don't know what you're talking about, girl," he mumbled looking away. He missed his chance to stand with Jesus in his darkest hour like he promised he would.

Twice more in that setting, Peter renounced any connection with Jesus. Then the rooster crowed. Suddenly, the Lord's words came rushing to his mind: "I tell you, Peter, before the rooster crows today, you will deny three times that you know me (Luke 22:34)." Peter looked up and there was Jesus. As their gaze met, the compassion in the Master's eyes cut him to the core. He ran from the scene and cried like he had never cried before. He had lost all hope. I identify with his painful regret for boldly saying one thing and shamefully acting the opposite.

Peter fades into the background during the rest of the crucifixion account in the Gospels. He appears in the narrative several times after the resurrection, such as when he went running in to see the empty tomb. He leaves without speaking to Jesus, and no conversations between Jesus and Peter are mentioned, although the Master does instruct Mary to tell His disciples and Peter that He is alive.

Peter was so discouraged and hopeless after denying his faith in Jesus that he decided to return to life as a fisherman, the life he knew before the Master called him to be a "fisher of men." Several of the disciples joined him, but their nets were empty as they headed back to shore.

"Did you catch anything for breakfast?" they heard across the water. Peter could see the outline of a man on the beach and the glow of a camp fire.

"No, we didn't," they replied.

"Throw the net on the other side and see what happens," he told them.

Something about the intonation of the voice reminded him of the Master. Then, when they felt the weight of the nets, Peter knew that it was Jesus. He jumped out of the boat and swam to the shore. He wanted to talk to Jesus and tell him how sorry he was for denying Him. Yet, once he was there, he simply stood close to the fire and warmed himself against the chilly morning air. Sorrow overwhelmed him as he recalled the last time he stood by a fire in the Lord's presence.

After breakfast, Jesus turned to Peter and said, "Do you love Me, Peter?"

Peter was not surprised by this question because he had failed Him miserably. "You know I love You," Peter replied with his head down.

"Then feed My lambs," Jesus said gently.

Jesus asked it again. "Peter, do you love Me?"

"Yes, Lord I really do care for You," replied Peter.

"Then become a good shepherd who compassionately takes care of those who blow it just like you did." And then a third time, Jesus asked the same question, "Peter, do you love Me?"

"Yes, Lord, I do care deeply for You," was his reply. This time he looked into the Master's eyes and saw the love and compassion there, which he needed.

"Then take care of the sheep and give them the message of hope you are receiving today."

In that moment, Peter looked beyond his failures and saw that he didn't have to be perfect and have all the answers. Instead, he needed to show how much he loved the Lord by caring for those who lost their way. He could show them the same compassion the Lord had shown him in his weakest moment.

Choosing to Trust

One Saturday afternoon as I was practicing worship songs for the Sunday service at our church, my husband came into the room with a shocked look on his face.

"I just got a call that Elizabeth has been in a serious accident," he said. "She's been taken to the hospital. They wouldn't give me many details on the phone."

We decided it would be best if I stayed home with our other two children until we knew more details. After he left, I attempted to go back to the worship songs I had picked. The main theme was the faithfulness of God.

"How much longer is this going to go on, Lord?" I cried out. "Will there ever be an end to this insanity? I'm not sure I can take any more."

For the first time, I was able to acknowledge my anger against God. I felt like He had let me down.

"Where are You, Lord? Why are You so distant? Why haven't You answered my prayers?" I shouted.

I didn't feel like worshipping, yet I pulled out the sheet music by Steve McEwan and forced myself to play.

Great is the Lord and most worthy of praise
The city of our God, the holy place
The joy of the whole earth
Great is the Lord in whom we have the victory
He aids us against the enemy
We bow down on our knees
And Lord, we want to lift Your name on high
And Lord, we want to thank You
For the works You've done in our lives
And Lord, we trust in Your unfailing love
For You alone are God eternal
Throughout earth and heaven above.

As I finished singing these words, I was overcome with tears of surrender. It's humbling to face your shortcomings, especially when they are as tangible as mine. I chose to lift the name of the Lord above the details of our situation. I chose to be grateful and trust that He was working. He had an eternal perspective that I could not see at the moment, but I could trust in His faithfulness and unchanging love regardless of what any of us did.

Do you ever wish you could go back and change a decision you've made? I certainly do. It can be hard to admit making a stupid decision like driving away from the scene of an accident. The worst part for me at the time was the sense of failure and disappointment in my parenting skills. I was ashamed to let people know how bad the situation was. At the root of it all, I felt like Elizabeth's problems were my fault. I accepted the blame for my daughter's choices. Her actions and my reactions were creating turmoil in our home. My husband and I argued about how to discipline her. Her siblings felt the tension from our constant fighting. It was like living in a war zone. I look back on this period of time in our lives with regret and sorrow. Recently I asked our other two children what they wished we had done differently.

"Mom, I just wish that we could have had family meetings where you and Dad would have told us everything that was going on," our younger daughter answered. "It was like we had this big secret that we were supposed to keep."

We were so consumed with dealing with Elizabeth's extreme rebellion that we didn't really talk openly about what was happening. At the time, we felt like we were protecting them, but they knew a lot was going on.

Our son expressed the same feeling. "As kids, we felt the same way you did, but I don't feel like it was ever acknowledged," he said. "I think it would have helped if you had given us more opportunities to express what we were going through. I took responsibility for my older sister and felt that if I could be really good, I could make it better."

Why was she so determined to go her own way and make our lives miserable? Do you hear that question? I was allowing our daughter to drive the family car and set the tone for our lives.

God is working in your situation even though outwardly it feels like everything is falling apart. As I look back on the car accidents Elizabeth had during this difficult time, I can see how the Lord was gently working in her heart through it all. He wanted her to learn valuable lessons through that first fender-bender. That didn't happen when I panicked and took the blame, shielding her from the consequences of her actions. He continued to protect her every step of the way in order to accomplish His purpose in her life. The last accident got her attention. She remembers crying out to God for help as she waited for the emergency crew to get her out of the wreck. What I thought was the end of the road actually was a wake-up call that she was not indestructible and needed to head back home.

I got back in the driver's seat as I regained confidence in the God's faithfulness to forgive me when I failed. As He restored my hope, I recognized that I was not expected to take this long journey alone. Instead of throwing my hands up and losing hope, I regained my confidence of the Lord's presence in every single predicament. Instead of relinquishing my leadership role in frustration, I got back in the driver's seat and steered our family in the right direction.

Hope Tools

ABC's of Hope

A sk for help. I missed many opportunities to receive support from those around me. I stayed hidden in the pain without asking for help because I was worried about what people would think and I didn't want to uncover the shame. My root issue was that I felt that Elizabeth's choices were somehow my fault. As I look back, I realize that I put my hope in her hands and gave her the keys to my well-being. People will pray with you if you only let them know you need help. Most importantly, ask the Lord for His protection and help. "Because he loves me," says the LORD, "I will rescue him; I will protect him, for he acknowledges my name. He will call on me, and I will answer him; I will be with him in trouble, I will deliver him and honor him. With long life I will satisfy him and show him my salvation (Psalm 91:14-16)."

B e realistic. Ignoring the problem about your current situation will not make it go away. Running from it only makes it worse. I made a poor choice when I panicked. The hardest part to face was that because I shouldered the blame for this accident, Elizabeth did not learn the lessons she could have learned at an earlier stage. I absorbed the pain and shame, and she was off the hook. Let your children accept the consequences for their actions because it will all come to light anyway. "There is nothing concealed that will not be disclosed, or hidden that will not be made known. What you have said in the dark will be heard in the daylight, and what you have whispered in the ear in the inner rooms will be proclaimed from the roofs (Luke 12:2-3)."

Concentrate on your circle of influence. It is important to recognize that you cannot control things that are outside your circle of influence. You must let go of the concerns that affect you. Instead, zero in on ways to stay calm no matter what your child does. Giving up my self-control allowed my emotions to escalate. I stopped thinking clearly and did things that I later regretted. Our situation turned around when I regained hope and focused on trusting that God was working on the inside despite what I saw externally. You will steer in the direction where you look, so keep your focus on the Lord. "If I keep my eyes on God, I won't trip over my own feet (Psalm 25:15 MSG)."

PRAYER

Lord, I ask that You guide me as I parent _____. You have promised to direct my steps when I put my trust in You. I acknowledge that I am at the end of my rope and don't know what else to do, yet I trust that You will set me on the right path (Proverbs 3:5-6). You are my rock and fortress. I put my confidence in Your strength and know that You will deliver us from trouble (Psalm 18:2).

As we go through tough times, I am so grateful that You are our defender when we look to You for our help (Psalm 121:1-2). I pray that _____ will call to You for help as she/he encounters trouble (Psalm 46:1). May she/he call upon Your name and experience the awareness of Your presence and comfort even in the dark and dangerous places of her/his life (Psalm 23:4).

I welcome You into our situation and receive Your peace from this time forward. This peace comes from You and not from our circumstances. Put a guard around my emotions and my mind through the power of Christ Jesus so I can remain calm no matter what happens (Philippians 4:6-7). Thank You for Your promises to continually work in _____'s life. I have great hope because I know You always keep Your Word (Hebrews 10:23 MSG).

I thank You that I can move forward in spite of what _____ chooses to do because I know that You are taking care of her/him. Even when I do not see any progress, I trust that in Your time we will get through these difficult days (Ecclesiastes 3:1).

In Jesus' name, Amen.

Hope Expressions

Always be prepared to give an answer to everyone who asks you to give the reason for the hope that you have. But do this with gentleness and respect.
I Peter 3:15

Using Your GPS
(Guiding Prayer Support)

I rocked slowly back and forth in the rocking chair, hoping the rhythmic movement would stop my racing mind so I could sleep. Our daughter, Elizabeth, eighteen years old at that time, had recently moved into an apartment with a friend. I tried to convince myself I had nothing to worry about. She seemed to be doing better lately. I wanted to trust her. She seemed happy, and everything looked okay from the outside. Still, I felt uneasy. My spirit was telling me to pray instead of going to bed. As I began to pray specific scriptural prayers for her, I started to feel more peaceful. Soon my body relaxed and my head nodded as I drifted off to sleep. I awoke with a start when I heard a woman's desperate cry for help.

I jumped up and ran to my mother-in-law's bedroom. She was sleeping soundly. Quietly I tip-toed back to my chair and resumed my prayer. I heard the cry a second time and ran to my other daughter's bedroom. She also was sound asleep. As I made my way back to the living room, I realized that I needed to pray for Elizabeth. I increased the intensity of prayer for her protection and most of all for her return to faith.

This was one of many sleepless nights during the dark times of our daughter's rebellion. A gradual change came as I started praying during these anxious times. In the beginning, I found myself praying in anger asking God to teach Elizabeth the lessons she needed to learn. My prayers reflected my hopelessness and despair. I am grateful that the Lord in His mercy didn't answer these angry prayers. This particular night, I was tempted to go back to my old pattern of pacing the floor in anxious despair, but instead I sat back down to personalize additional scriptures with Elizabeth's name. I lost track of time as I prayed through the verses. Finally a sense of peace settled over me, and I went to bed.

The next morning, Elizabeth called. She seemed very subdued, so I asked if she had time to hear about my experience the night before. As I told her how I realized I needed to pray for her, she started to cry. "Mom, can I move back home?" she pleaded.

"Of course you can, sweetie," I replied. This was the answer to many prayer sessions. I could tell that this time was different. I sensed a profound change in her. This was a turning point for Elizabeth.

It was not until later that I learned what had happened during that prayer session. At the precise moment that I heard the voice of a woman crying for help, she was in danger for her life, and when I began praying for her specifically, she felt a surge of supernatural strength that allowed her to get away to safety. I believe Elizabeth is alive today because of the intercession of her family. This was one instance where we know God spared her life. I am certain there were others as she placed herself in many dangerous situations with gangs, drugs, and the occult.

Your Prayers Make a Difference

It's easy to give up hope and think there is nothing you can do when your child turns from his or her faith. However, the truth is you have a powerful role as you consistently pray and believe that the Lord is faithfully at work. Many of us reserve prayer for times of crisis or for general protection as we fall asleep at night, but God is calling us to focused prayer for the next generation. Ezekiel 22:30 says that God is looking for those who will do something about the breaches in the wall and 'stand in the gap' on behalf of others. This refers to the walls that protected a city. The enemies of those within the walls looked for holes to storm through in order to take the city. In a spiritual sense, the enemy wants to storm in and destroy our children. As parents, we can pray and stand in the gap through focused intercession for our children. If you see a widening gap, it's time to place one hand on the promises in God's Word and the other on your child. Pray for wisdom and spiritual understanding (Colossians 1:9).

PRAY THE SCRIPTURES

Part of my journey in returning to hope was to read the Bible with a different perspective. I started looking for promises that I could appropriate for my family. Biblically-based prayers are powerful, especially if you personalize them. In the first place, your faith grows as you read the Word of God (Romans 10:17). Also, you remove negative emotions and hopelessness from the prayer equation.

You declare the truth of what God wants to accomplish in your child. You are praying according to His will, and He promises to answer. The book that helped me during this difficult time was Stormie Omartian's book, *The Power of a Praying Parent,* because it uses Biblically-based prayers.

One of the first changes that came about through praying scripture was that I began to treat my daughter with the hope that came as a gift from the Lord. Grace is available for us as we go through trials, if we will take it. The more I prayed the truth and personalized it with Elizabeth's name, the more hope grew in my heart, and the more I was able to communicate this to her.

As I began looking for scriptures that expressed blessings for future generations, I was amazed to discover how far the blessings extended. A very special passage in Isaiah 54:13-14 became a cornerstone for my prayers. I approached this verse first as a personal prayer for peace and righteousness. Then I circled back and prayed, putting Elizabeth's name in the verse as follows: "Elizabeth shall be taught by the Lord, and great will be her peace. She is established in righteousness. She is not oppressed. She will not fear and terror will not come near her." I needed that reassurance and affirmation that the Lord's peace replaced fear and terror in our lives—especially at this difficult time.

WEAVE PRAYER INTO DAILY ROUTINES

Pray consistently. Make the commitment to pray on a daily basis for the spiritual growth of your children. Let this prayer time take the highest priority even if you are in a panic about where your child is headed.

Prayer can become a way of life and a thread that brings the light of hope into every area of your family's life. "You have made known to me the ways of life. You will make me full of joy in your presence (Acts 2:28)." You don't have to be in church to pray. You can pray as you clean the house, work in the yard, drive to and from work and anywhere else you may be. You can trust that even your darkest hours are glorious opportunities to see God's power at work.

When prayer is based on the love that God gives us for our children, hope comes alive. Faith-filled scriptural prayers inspire love and positive results. "Hope does not disappoint, because the love of God has been poured out in our hearts by the Holy Spirit who was given to us (Romans 5:5)."

Keep a Prayer Journal

The journal doesn't have to be fancy—just a place for you to record the scriptures, the prayers, and the answers. Habakkuk 2:2 says to "write down the revelation and make it plain." Be sure to write the date when you pray the request and go back and write down the answers so it can become a praise journal when you are in the middle of a storm. When you look back, you will be encouraged to see how far they have come and how many miracles have occurred.

Keep Praying

How do you find the strength to keep praying if you are not seeing any answers and it seems like your child continues to go the wrong direction? You trust that God is working even when you don't see immediate results. This is when you receive the gift of hope so you can walk by faith and not by sight. Don't give up on what God has promised to do. Pray for everyone involved to become stronger in their faith. God is working under the surface even when you cannot see anything on the outside. In Ephesians 6:18 we are encouraged to: "Pray in the Spirit on all occasions with all kinds of prayers and requests.

With this in mind, be alert and always keep on praying for all the Lord's people."

Praise More

Start your prayer time by focusing on the positive things that the Lord has been doing in your life. Praise Him for who He is and thank Him for His promises to hear and answer your prayers. Your perspective changes as you declare the truth about God and how He sees your child. It is possible to go from complaining about your situation to praising God for completing the process. He always finishes what He starts (Philippians 1:6). The change in our situation was gradual yet effective. I experienced so much more peace, which enabled me to sleep at night and cope during the day. Many other things were going on in our lives at that specific time, but this was one area where I was able to place Elizabeth in the Lord's hands and leave her there. It's the best position for your prodigal—in the loving arms of their Heavenly Father. His consistent, loving approach makes all the difference.

Hope Tools

GPS

Guidance: When you feel lost in the journey with your prodigal, turn on your GPS. If you don't know what to do with your child, pray and ask the Lord for guidance. James 1:5 says that if anyone feels like they lack wisdom, they simply need to ask for it. The good news is that God promises to give His perspective liberally when we humbly approach Him. He doesn't find fault with us when we ask for help. In fact, He loves for us to ask Him for what we need. So many times, I asked and followed the advice of other parents only to make matters worse. There is a better way. Listen carefully to the guidance that comes from the Lord as He shows you the direction to go (Isaiah 30:21).

Prayer: In difficult times, we can talk a lot about praying yet may not actually pray. Begin praying intentional, focused scripture-based prayers. Your faith will grow as you align your requests with the Word of God. Every time you feel desperate, turn to God who is your source of hope and faith. As a parent, you have a unique position of spiritual authority in your child's life. Use prayer to establish a life-giving environment where your child can return to faith. Your prayers make a difference because as it says in James 5:16, "The prayer of a righteous man (or woman) is powerful and effective."

Support: Call in reinforcements. I recommend Moms in Prayer (formerly Moms in Touch), an outstanding organization that facilitates prayer with other parents and grandparents. They have local chapters all across the country and even internationally. Their approach is to pray scripturally for each other's children. Great resources can be found on their website at www.momsinprayer.org, making it simple even for those who have no experience praying in group settings. Also, you can find guidance on starting a group yourself. No matter what you are going through, you can know that God will show up as you join others in prayer (Matthew 18:20). A strong prayer support group makes a huge difference in the journey. "He has delivered us from such a deadly peril, and he will deliver us again. On him we have set our hope that he will continue to deliver us, as you help us by your prayers. Then many will give thanks

on our behalf for the gracious favor granted us in answer
to the prayers of many (2 Corinthians 1:10-11)."

PRAYER

Thank You, Lord, for teaching me how to pray effec-
tively for _____. I am so grateful that You are willing
to do more than I could ever ask or think on her/his behalf.
I believe that You are working powerfully inside her/him
even when it might not show externally (Ephesians 4:20).
Give me courage and strength to continue to pray for her/
him and to not be shaken. Reveal Your power to her/him
and show her/him Your path of life. May she/he find
joy in Your presence and the pleasure of knowing You
(Psalm 16:8-11).

Thank You for doing more that I could ever ask or
imagine. I know You are working in _____ in order
to reveal Your glory and purpose and also to bless future
generations (Ephesians 4:20-21).

Lord, open _____'s eyes so that she/he may turn
from darkness to light and from the dominion of Satan to
God, in order that she/he may receive forgiveness of sins
and an inheritance among those who have been sanctified
by faith in You (Acts 26:18). I pray that she/he will know

You in a deeper way than ever before. May she/he run to You rather than from You (Psalm 7:1).

Thank You for sending the Spirit of truth to guide _____ into all the truth that You have for her/him (John 16:13). Place within her/him a desire to read Your Word and to seek the truth. This truth will set her/him free (John 8:32). Thank You that You will listen as she/he calls upon You and prays to You. As she/he seeks You, she/he will find You (Jeremiah 29:12-13).

In Jesus' name I pray, Amen.

Hope Expressions

Then you will call upon Me and come and pray to Me, and I will listen to you. And you will seek Me and find Me when you search for Me with all your heart.
Jeremiah 29:12-13 (NASB)

Planning the Welcome Home Party

The young man awoke with a start. He had just had a vivid dream that he was back home. He was sitting around the table with his parents and older brother. A feast was set before them, and warmth and laughter filled the room. However, the delicious aroma of food quickly gave way to the stench of the pigpen as the young man returned to reality. Slowly, he stretched the sore muscles in his back and stumbled over to the pig feed. He was so hungry, he would have gladly eaten some of it, but he was hired to feed it to the swine. As he threw it over the fence, he thought, "What am I doing here? The servants at home are comfortable and at least have food to eat. I'm going home."

There are no details as to how long the prodigal son was away. The only information we have is that he went to a foreign country and blew through his inheritance very quickly. He scattered it to the wind and spent it recklessly with no restraints. When hard times came, he had no savings or resources to fall back on. All his friends abandoned him once he ran out of money, and he felt like he had burned all the bridges leading home. He found himself in a strange place with no place to stay, no money, and no skills to earn a living.

On his way home, the prodigal son rehearsed his speech. He was pretty good at convincing people and getting them to go his way. At least he used to be. Tears ran down his face as he remembered the sorrow in his father's eyes when he left. "I was just so foolish to leave like that," he chided himself. Every step he took closer to home caused the knot in his stomach to grow tighter. "What if my father turns his back on me and tells me that he has disowned me?" he thought. He felt so ashamed of his failures. "I'm going to beg for a job. I have learned a lot about hard work since I've been gone."

WATCHING AND WAITING

Every day the distinguished man sat at the city gates with a sense of expectation. Even as he spoke to the other city leaders, he continually scanned the incoming crowds for a familiar silhouette.

"You know, there are those who think that I'm a foolish old man to continue to believe that my son will return," he said to the men around him.

They looked away so he would not see the pity in their eyes. This godly man had actually given his rebellious son his blessing as the young man left with his share of the inheritance. It was hard to understand how this father could have such a deep love for an undeserving, undisciplined son.

"There are those who say I should move on and give him up for dead, yet I know he will come home. In fact, I was speaking to the servants about the welcome home party that we will have when he arrives," he continued. "When that day comes, I want all of you to know that you are invited. We are going to have a wonderful time!"

He never said a word against his son. He was at peace and filled with hope.

"I can't wait to sit down and talk with him about all that he has learned while he's been gone. He always was a stubborn one—had to learn things the hard way," he continued. The father smiled as he remembered past conversations with his strong-willed son. "One thing's for sure though, you always know where you stand with him," he said quietly as his eyes shone with unshed tears.

Grace Reunites

As the young man looked up, he saw the silhouette of his town. He had made it! The long walk had been hard enough, but nothing compared to facing his father who had every right to disown him. He looked up briefly and saw a man running toward him. He squinted against the setting sun to see who was running. It was his father! Fear gripped his heart! It could only mean one thing—his father was angry. He almost turned around but decided to stay the course and resolve this issue.

Finally, he was face-to-face with the man who had given him so much. He grabbed his father's hand and knelt on the ground. He couldn't bring himself to make eye contact because he was so ashamed. "Father, I have sinned against both heaven and you and I am no longer worthy of being called your son. Please take me on as a hired servant (Luke 15:18-19 NLT)."

Gently, the father reached down and lifted his son's chin until he was forced to look at him. Bending close, he kissed his cheek, pulled him to his feet, and enfolded him in a warm hug—a hug that dissolved the fear that had been gnawing in the young man's stomach. The warmth of mercy and grace coming from his godly father caused the son's reserves of self-effort to melt. He leaned into the warmth and strength of his father. He couldn't believe that coming home had been so simple. It was not the complicated process that he had built up in his mind because mercy and grace had covered his sin. He didn't have to be perfect. He just needed to be up front and willing to grow up.

His father hugged him again and looked at him with tears in his eyes. "I knew you would come home," he said. "So I've been planning your 'welcome home' party for a long time."

The young man could not believe it. He felt unworthy, yet knew he was right where he belonged. His position was not based on his performance, but rather on his relationship with his loving father.

Hope Rays

It takes hope to plan a party when your child is far from the Lord and living a lifestyle you cannot approve. There doesn't seem much to celebrate when you struggle to sleep and feel empty inside. Who wants to party when you feel like that? My symptoms of hope deprivation had become so 'normal' that I didn't realize how dark my outlook was until I received the instructions to 'paint a picture of hope.' I had set a background of doom and gloom in my attempt to get Elizabeth to change her behaviors. It backfired because she felt she had gone too far with no hope of returning. My focus had been on dangerous behaviors and externals. Negative thinking became my normal way of approaching the situation. The last thing on my mind was planning her welcome home party.

On the way home from work one gloomy day, I reflected on how nothing seemed to be working or changing in Elizabeth's life. The dark clouds in the sky matched how I felt inside. I started sobbing and finally had to pull the car over to the side of the road.

"Lord, I just don't have anything extra to give. You told me to establish an atmosphere of hope for Elizabeth. I thought by now things would be different. Where am I going to find the paint that I need to paint her a picture of hope?" I cried.

Shortly after, I looked up at the sky and saw a dark cloud that looked like a painter had outlined it with brilliant iridescent, gold paint. Streams of light radiated from behind the cloud and reached toward earth. It was so beautiful that I got out of my car to enjoy it more completely. That's when it dawned on me. The sun shines faithfully behind the darkest clouds. It is not up to me to try to manufacture sunshine or make everything turn out the way it should be. I can't produce hope on my own or make others change. I didn't need for everything to turn around before I could start painting. I only needed hope to see the bright outline around the current dark clouds. The steadfast love of the Lord was shining from behind the dark cloud. He had not gone anywhere. He was still shining brightly. His mercy and kindness would never fail.

I can celebrate, knowing that the sun is still shining behind dark clouds even when I can't see it. I can appreciate the brightness of the beautiful rays of sunlight in contrast to the dark clouds.

REFRAME

To reframe is to take a step back and change focus. I can step back and see that even when our situation has not changed and, in fact, may be getting worse, God is unchanging. He is the constant provider of all that we need. He is the eternal provider of hope and perspective.

If your prodigal is still far from home, you can know that God is at work behind the dark clouds that seem to engulf you. If you have given up, now is the time to start planning the welcome home party so that you are ready when the time comes. It's an ongoing exercise of trust and faith. The New Living Translation (NLT) of Hebrews 11:1 says, "Faith is the confidence that what we hope for will actually happen; it gives us assurance about things we cannot see."

The parable includes no details about what happened after the lost son came home other than the problem with his brother. Yet from that brief dialogue, we understand that life wasn't suddenly rosy. I feel that tidbit was included to encourage us as we open our hearts to the prodigals and welcome them home. Things can get messy sometimes, yet as we continue to place our hope and trust in the Lord, He provides grace and strength to overcome each challenge.

No matter where your child is right now, begin to plan the welcome home party. Hope fills you with the possibilities of how you will celebrate when your dear one comes to his or her senses. I don't know what's going on in your family right now, but I do know that we serve an amazing God who is ready to fill you with hope for the future. He will heal the hurts, restore relationships, and strengthen your entire family. Celebrate the amazing destiny wrapped around the gifts and talents of your child. Open your arms wide to hug him or her and convey the unconditional love that you have received from God. Invite the Lord to the party because He rejoices when those who are lost decide to come home. He will stand guard over your celebration and bring peace to your family (Psalm 5:11-12 MSG).

Hope Tools

Party Plans

Perspective: In the panorama of Elizabeth's life, this was a difficult season, but not the end. The problems felt overwhelming, but they were never intended to destroy us. They were intended to make us stronger in our faith and in our relationships with God and one another. When I looked up, I could see a sliver of light shooting from behind the dark cloud that had hung over us for so long. It's all in your focus. You can either say, "These are the darkest times of our lives. This is terrible. This should not be happening to us." Or, you can say, "This has been a difficult chapter in our family's story and we have come through stronger, with a greater measure of compassion and with a strong testimony of God's grace."

If the clouds are dark and menacing, continue to believe that the sun is shining behind them. The breathtaking rays of light that shoot through the dark clouds are outstanding because of their contrast. Get out the camera and take some pictures of the glory of the light coming from behind the dark cloud. Breakthroughs are coming soon despite the dark clouds that seem to envelop you.

Anticipating: When dealing with a rebellious child, you can either let your mind run away with catastrophic endings or pinpoint the good outcome God has promised. Apprehension seems to come instinctively as you face the reality of your child's choices. I was in no mood to buy party supplies when I was sick with worry about the outcome of our situation. It takes a gift of faith to expect a good result and to zero in on the positive results that will come as you continue to pray fervently and speak words of hope.

As you seek God's face and pray for your child to find his or her purpose in life, you will be filled with a different type of anticipation. This is not about superficial changes, but rather about believing that every experience he or she encounters is yet another area where God is working.

Relaxing: It is possible to have peace in the midst of this tumultuous journey. Take time to relax and enjoy the present moment. There is comfort in knowing that you are ready to receive your child with open arms when he or she comes home. Right now you have an opportunity to gain your composure and be confident that the party will happen. Psalm 116:7 says, "Relax and rest for God has showered you with blessings (MSG)."

It's a miracle to be able to relax before you see the desired results. It's the revelation of hope that changes the atmosphere from tension to peace. Enjoy the quiet because you'll be having a loud party soon!

Turning: The parable of the prodigal son shows us the heart of our Heavenly Father. The prodigal's father is turned toward his son from the beginning. He waits patiently for his son's heart to be turned toward home. Scripture says that, when he was starving, the undisciplined and dissipated young man came to his senses and realized that the good life was back at home where even the servants ate three square meals a day. As he made plans to head back home, he started rehearsing a speech that would surely capture his father's attention. He would ask for a job because he knew that would please his father. Besides, he was hungry and the most practical thing to do was to return home. The young man considered the possibilities of what could happen once he got there. He knew he had done wrong.

Even though mentally he was headed in the right direction, his heart had not yet been completely restored. When he saw his father running toward him, the last reserve melted. His father had been waiting for him to come home. Then when his father hugged and kissed him, he began to weep. True repentance flowed from the mercy his father had for him. He could once again hope for a bright future. That is something worth celebrating!

Yielding: As a parent of a young adult, you have to come to terms with the fact that you must abandon your control. That is actually a great thing to celebrate. While it may be scary in the beginning as you recognize the dangers out there, hope helps you to see the foundation of a different relationship with your offspring. You can look forward with joy, knowing that as they move into another level of maturity, you can become friends. As one of my friends put it, "It's amazing how much I learned from the time my daughter was 16 until she turned 21." It's time to party because of the fact that as one stage of your parenting has come to an end, another is beginning. The future is bright and filled with hope.

Our Heavenly Father is showing us a path of grace, compassion, and love. It's never too late to celebrate.

There's always room on the grill and a place at the table to celebrate the return to faith and family.

Prayer

Thank You, Lord, for showing me a better way to parent. I start by praising and celebrating all that You are doing. You've already done your share of miracles and You have a solid, well-thought-out plan for _____ (Isaiah 25:1 MSG). Please give me wisdom as I plan for our future celebration. You have promised to give it generously (James 1:5). Allow me to be a conduit of Your love to _____. I want to love her/him the way You love me—unconditionally and extravagantly (Ephesians 5:1-2 MSG). Teach me what that love looks like. I will look to Your example and will continue to prepare the 'welcome home' party. Show me ways to celebrate small victories and to release _____ to learn every lesson You want him/her to learn during this time. I thank You that I can have peace no matter what she/he chooses.

I pray that as _____ comes home she/he will recognize that we celebrate the gifts and the life she/he brings to us. Help _____ to realize that she/he is a blessing to us and a vital part of our family. We celebrate her/him and who she/he is. We celebrate the day she/he was born. If _____ doesn't feel that right now, I ask You show her/him the things that she/he does well. Reveal to her/him all the unique talents that You placed within her/him when You created her/him. I am grateful for the amazing destiny that is wrapped up in who she/he is. May _____ be comfortable in that and have nothing to prove. I pray for rest, joy, and peace as she/he comes home.

Lord, we invite You to our party because we know that You rejoice when those who are lost decide to come home. Stand guard over our celebration and bring peace to our family (Psalm 5:11-12).

In Jesus' name, Amen.

Hope Expressions

'We're going to have a wonderful time! My son is here— given up for dead and now alive! Given up for lost and now found!' And they began to have a wonderful time.
Luke 15:23-24 ~ The Message

Afterword

ELIZABETH'S VIEWPOINT

I knew Mom was writing a book about the rebellious time in my life. It was a really hard time for our family. When we read it together, both of us cried. It makes me sad but at the same time glad that I am still alive. I recently realized how much I've grown since the days that Mom writes about in this book.

A few weeks ago, I had to go before a judge because of an unpaid traffic ticket that had gone to warrant. As I stood in line, tears began to stream down my face and I couldn't stop them. I was so emotional because it hit me that this could have been my life. Since I turned myself in and I had no prior record, I was able to pay the rest

PREPARE THE WAY HOME

of my fine and go home to my wonderful husband and amazing sons.

Prayer really does make a difference. I am grateful for all those who prayed for me during this time of my life: my parents, grandparents, aunts and uncles, and my church family. I am thankful for all those who reached out to me and loved me unconditionally.

I would like to tell parents who have a rebellious child, "Don't give up!" No matter what I did, my parents were always there. They didn't force their beliefs on me. They just loved me and believed in me even though I was making wrong decisions.

Love your child unconditionally. People make stupid choices, but we shouldn't shut them out because of the mistakes they have made. Don't give up on them. You can disagree with what they're doing, yet at the same time let them know that you love them.

When people do change, families need to change themselves. The past is the past. We all need to move forward and not let the relationship suffer. I know that when trust is broken, it can be hard to repair. At the same time, hope says that tomorrow is a new day. I'm so glad my family gave me the gift of hope so that I could move forward.

My Dad bought me a little bracelet when I was in kindergarten. It had our address on one side. The other side had a little Precious Moments shepherd with his staff at the top and Psalm 23 beneath it. I never forgot that. No matter how tough I seemed outwardly, there was a soft place in my heart for what I had been taught. My Dad used to tell me, "Elizabeth, you look tough on the outside, but inside—you're just 50 cent putty. You can run all you want from God, but you have so many people praying for you that you don't have a chance to get too far."

I am so happy to say that this scripture is now true:

"God, my shepherd! I don't need a thing. You have bedded me down in lush meadows, you find me quiet pools to drink from. True to your word, you let me catch my breath and send me in the right direction. Even when the way goes through Death Valley, I'm not afraid when you walk at my side. Your trusty shepherd's crook makes me feel secure. You serve me a six-course dinner right in front of my enemies. You revive my drooping head; my cup brims with blessing. Your beauty and love chase after me every day of my life. I'm back home in the house of God for the rest of my life." ~ Psalm 23 ~ The Message

It's good to be home.

About the Author

Karen Sebastian was born to Bill and Betty Pritchett and spent most of her childhood on the mission field where she saw lives transformed through the hope of Jesus Christ. Karen met her husband, Bill Sebastian, at Pacific Life College where they both trained for ministry. Together, Karen and Bill served on the mission field in Central America, and later as pastors in California and Texas, bringing hope to thousands as they faithfully ministered the Gospel of Jesus Christ to the Church and in the marketplace.

After enduring the heartache of infertility, the Sebastians were blessed with the gift of adopting a precious baby girl and later giving birth to two biological children. The Lord used the transforming power of hope to powerfully impact their lives as they raised their three children and to persevere through a painful journey to see their prodigal come home. Because of this, Karen became known as "The Hope Lady" as she began using her gifts to speak hope into the lives of others. Today Karen continues to minister hope to thousands in conferences, writings, and through her company, HOPEpreneurs.

The Sebastians live in Grand Prairie, Texas, and are the proud grandparents of five amazing boys. They treasure moments with family and always hold fast to hope.